HEALTHCARE WARRIORS

HEALTHCARE WARRIORS

Why and How to Become One

Dr. Ira Williams

Copyright © 2022 Dr. Ira Williams.

All rights reserved. No part of this book may be reproduced, stored, or transmitted by any means—whether auditory, graphic, mechanical, or electronic—without written permission of both publisher and author, except in the case of brief excerpts used in critical articles and reviews. Unauthorized reproduction of any part of this work is illegal and is punishable by law.

ISBN: 979-8-88640-406-7 (sc)
ISBN: 979-8-88640-407-4 (hc)
ISBN: 979-8-88640-408-1 (e)

Because of the dynamic nature of the Internet, any web addresses or links contained in this book may have changed since publication and may no longer be valid. The views expressed in this work are solely those of the author and do not necessarily reflect the views of the publisher, and the publisher hereby disclaims any responsibility for them.

One Galleria Blvd., Suite 1900, Metairie, LA 70001
1-888-421-2397

CONTENTS

Introduction 7

Chapter 1: How to become a Healthcare Warrior 15

Chapter 2: Why become a Healthcare Warrior 20

Chapter 3: One State's Current System 33

Chapter 4: The Bridge 40

Chapter 5: How It All Began 42

Chapter 6: 1800 – 1900 Growing Pains 47

Chapter 7: 1900 – 1950 Early Development of a System 56

Chapter 8: Dawn of Modern Medicine 65

Chapter 9: Quality of Care Army of Experts 75

Chapter 10: What Other Experts Are Saying 91

Conclusion 123

About Dr. Williams 131

My Books 133

INTRODUCTION

Healthcare and **Education** are two of the greatest responsibilities the leaders and decision-makers of each state owe to their fellow citizens, and sadly, every governor and state legislator, past and present, have failed miserably in their combined efforts to fulfill those responsibilities. While Education holds the key for future success in life for every individual Healthcare directly impacts each individual's life beginning with the moment of conception and extending until their last breathe is taken.

Healthcare, the word, implies multiple connotations; one's individual health as determined both by their personal behavior, and the degree of medical care they receive during the course of a medical need. Healthcare also denotes the far greater concept of service to an entire community, state, and nation. Healthcare is one of the most dominating characteristics of every nation, and yet every nation's current Healthcare System can be found to be sorely lacking in its ability to adequately, and uniformly serve its citizens. More significantly, there are clearly evident reasons why each nation's, and where possible, each nation's states fall far short of achieving the goal of being able to provide an adequate system here in the second decade of the 21st Century.

People at every level within the current system of healthcare are forced to acknowledge "their system is broken". And "broken" is such a poor word for such an important understanding. The current Healthcare Delivery System is now, and has always been, disorganized, and highly dysfunctional and in spite of the collective efforts by an enormous army of quality of healthcare and patient safety experts seeking to improve that "system" for the past several decades the following two latest summations illustrate the dire status of the current Healthcare Delivery System throughout the nation.

Medical errors are the 3rd leading cause of deaths in the U.S. following only heart disease and cancer.

Every new estimate of needless hospital deaths has been greater than all previous estimates for the past 28 years.

How could one of the nation's, and each state's, greatest responsibilities to every citizen evolve into such an unorganized and dysfunctional entitlements? And more importantly, how can the Federal and each state's collection of decision makers be forced to recognize the failures of the current system, and begin a process necessary to create a 21st century Healthcare Delivery System worthy of that label?

Healthcare Warriors offer the best opportunity for creating the necessary energy to begin to force state lawmakers to recognize their responsibility and take action. The Healthcare Delivery System is primarily a state responsibility, and state legislators best respond to organized and collective demands, thus the urgent need for a sufficiently organized group of individuals seeking to demand meaningful change.

The target of this book are those individuals who are aware of the obvious shortcomings of their state's current Healthcare Delivery System because they have experienced various forms of some of those short comings, and who are willing to join in a unified effort to make a difference where they and their loved ones live.

Why are **Healthcare Warriors** so vitally important to any effort to create a 21st century Healthcare Delivery System within their state?

Two Greatest Mistakes

1. **States** are responsible to create and maintain an effective Healthcare Delivery System.

3 Fundamental Facts:
All medical care is local.
States license doctors, hospitals, and surgery centers.
All 50 state medical examining boards are over 100 years old and each board has a mission statement containing the phrase, "to regulate the practice of medicine."

I consider those first two facts to be "joined at the hip", meaning they should always be considered jointly, and those three facts should be sufficient for recognizing each state's responsibility to create and maintain an effective Healthcare Delivery System. Yet none of the Quality of Care & Patient Safety experts who have been promising great improvements in the multiple Federal Agencies, foundations, think tanks, etc. ever talk about each state's responsibility to create and maintain an effective Healthcare Delivery System. It is my belief that it will be impossible to ever even begin to create a 21st century Healthcare Delivery System until and unless everyone recognizes each state's responsibility.

The failure to recognize each state's responsibility to create and maintain an effective Healthcare Delivery System is one of the two greatest mistakes regarding that aspect of the nation's Healthcare System, its Delivery System (doctors & hospitals).

2. **The "System"** is a **Non-System** is the other great mistake regarding the Healthcare Delivery System, and that critical understanding has been recognized for over two decades by the experts within the multiple Federal agencies created to improve the quality of care and patient safety, and yet that critical understanding has been thoroughly ignored. Every state has a Healthcare Delivery System comprised of multiple components,

but every state's system is devoid of any systematic characteristics. The word *system* implies multiple components of an entity acting jointly in a systematic manner. In reality, each state's current Healthcare Delivery System components act as if they each speak a different language. Still, it is impossible for anyone to speak at any length about "Healthcare" without being compelled to use the word *system*, and without knowing that each use of that word demonstrates a complete lack of understanding.

I have challenged Quality of Care & Patient Safety experts in several of the Federal Agencies that have been created during the past decades regarding those "mistakes", and my challenges have always fallen on deaf ears. But there has never been any attempt to refute my challenges. And there is one more Fundamental Understanding that needs to be well understood prior to any attempt to begin to create a 21st century Healthcare Delivery System at state level.

Healthcare's Two Aspects

Our nation's Healthcare System has two equally important aspects that are equally flawed, but are as different as boys and girls, and their differences must be fully recognized and treated differently.

Cost & Access (how to pay for healthcare after-the-fact):
Very important and the aspect of healthcare that receives the vast majority of legislative and media attention with the focus on ObamaCare, RomneyCare, ClintonCare, Medicare, Medicaid, insured, uninsured, etc. The seemingly never-ending battle between those who want (demand) a Federal Single-Payer System, and those strongly opposed to that form of how to pay for healthcare after-the-fact.

But assume a miracle. A genius has provided a perfect system for how to pay for healthcare after-the-fact that is acceptable to everyone. Nothing will have changed in any state's Healthcare Delivery System and that is where the "rubber meets the road" in the delivery of care, and that is also where individual patient care falls through the cracks in that non-system. That is also where potential Healthcare Warriors come face-to-face with the broken aspects of the current non-system.

States are responsible for the Healthcare Delivery System and every state's current Healthcare Delivery System is "broken", and has always been broken.

Healthcare Warriors are the best solution for how to begin to force every state governor and state legislator to recognize their failure to fulfill their responsibility to create and maintain an effective Healthcare Delivery System. I have been trying to talk with Legislators in South Carolina for the past eight years about how I have been able to recognize the fundamental problems within our state's current Healthcare Delivery System as I was writing my books on that subject. And until recently due to a major event that has taken place involving the Greenville Health System of Greenville SC, state legislators have been oblivious to the problems of that so-called system, but more on that later.

The Subject is YOUR Healthcare Delivery System

People need to understand that when experts say, "the healthcare system is broken" they are talking about Your and Your Loved Ones' Healthcare Delivery System (doctors, hospitals, and surgery centers). Becoming a patient in any hospital in America is like shooting craps in Las Vegas, not everyone comes out a winner. The vast majority of all medical care is acceptable, and much of it is exceptional. The problem arises when any patient care falls short of being acceptable, or my preferred term *questionable patient care*. If enough people want a better Healthcare Delivery System, they need to become sufficiently organized to begin to demand meaningful change from those who were elected to create such change.

As a board certified oral & maxillofacial surgeon and anesthesiologist I have seen first hand the terrible consequences when medical care falls far short of its intended goal. I have served as a hospital medical staff department chairman, and member of the hospital medical staff executive committee, and as president of my state's specialty organization. But my understanding of the failures of any state's Healthcare Delivery System goes far beyond those positions of responsibility. I have testified in court as an expert witness against other medical surgeons in the city in which I practiced. And I paid the price for breaking the "code of silence", and being economically forced to sell my home and relocate. But my heretical behavior within my local medical community also provided me with sufficient understanding to be able to write three books on the failures within our current Healthcare Delivery System. I knew there would be a price to pay when I accepted the responsibility to testify in detail as the second surgeon to the negligent care provided by the first surgeon involving negligent patient care at all three of the private hospitals in Madison Wisconsin several decades ago. I testified against other doctors within my community because not doing so would have led me to becoming one of them, and I have never regretted my decision.

First Do No Harm, The Cure for Medical Malpractice was self-published in 2004, and it recounts some details of the multiple cases of negligent patient care I assumed the responsibility to surgically correct, and far more detail on how the medical profession has always failed in their duty to protect the public from those few doctors who are responsible for much of the patient harm that has always been a part of the Healthcare Delivery System. And I will provide more details regarding the professional failures of that "profession" later in the book because that factor is an integral part of why the Healthcare Delivery System has always been "broken".

Medical malpractice, and even the cure, are not topics of high interest in the book-selling market place, but the months of researching and writing that book captivated my interest in seeking a greater understanding of that aspect of Healthcare that I had dedicated most of my life to, and I began to search for, and gather information from multiple sources. However, being technologically limited (to say the least), I obtained the services of a person who was self-employed writing on the internet. I was blessed, because she suggested that I seek an opportunity to share my new-found insights regarding the many shortcomings of the current system by requesting to present a series of talks at a local university's senior learning-in-retirement program. I requested, and they accepted, and I presented a series of talks that were far more beneficial to me than apparently to my audience. My small audience of senior citizens did not respond well to my offerings, and I was not invited back for future presentations, but the process of compiling my information in a suitable manner for multiple presentations led me to far greater insight, and the desire to write my second book.

Misdiagnosed, Why Current Health Care Change is Malpractice was self-published in 2010, and I believe it is the first attempt ever made to depict the organizational structure of a state's Healthcare Delivery System, namely South Carolina's system where I live. I thought then, and continue to think, that my effort, regardless of how flawed one might consider it, might inspire someone else to think, "A good idea, but I can write a better book on that subject." As far as I can tell that book and my third book are the only books to attempt to describe in some detail any state's Healthcare Delivery System, and that is regrettable.

2010 is the pivotal year that began the process that has led me to recognizing the vital importance of the following series of understandings:

- States are where meaningful change in the current Healthcare Delivery System must take place.
- It will be impossible to even begin to create a 21st century Healthcare Delivery System without fully recognizing each state's responsibility.
- Governors and State Legislators are the only persons who can enact such change, but I have found that talking to Governors and State Legislators about a subject that they have NO understanding is like talking to a door.

- Thus, the need for Healthcare Warriors who can become far more understanding of the flaws in the current system, and the critical need for meaningful change, and who will develop an attitude that those Warriors will not take NO for an answer.

This book is an open invitation to those individuals who have recognized first hand the many flaws in the current system, and may have wished that there might be some way for them to become actively engaged in a process to make things better. I can promise such individuals two things; I am qualified to provide them with far more details about why the current system is broken, and how to be able to gain an understanding that will easily surpass the current understanding of their state's political leaders. I can also guarantee them that my support for their effort will be a labor of love for me because I have become convinced that such an organization as Healthcare Warriors can be the "game-changer" so desperately needed. Every state's current Healthcare Delivery System is broken, and any attempt to try to fix those systems would be futile. President Kennedy said that American men should be the first men to walk on the moon and return safely, and our nation did that. A similar process is necessary to begin to create a 21st century Healthcare Delivery System in every state, and Healthcare Warriors can lead the way.

CHAPTER 1

How to become a Healthcare Warrior

Healthcare Warriors unfortunately are primarily created by they or a loved one becoming part of the current Healthcare Delivery System collateral damage. I repeat, most medical care is acceptable, and much of it is exceptional in by far the greatest Healthcare Delivery System in the World. But all doctors are human, and all humans make mistakes, therefore all doctors make mistakes. Problem is that even though they are relatively few in number, a very high percentage of those anticipated patient care mistakes are being made by a relatively few practitioners. And members of the medical profession have never, throughout their entire history, ever been diligent in identifying and controlling, or when necessary, expelling those members of that profession that demonstrate an inability to provide their patient care in an acceptable manner. Doctors do not know how to judge other doctors regarding questionable patient care, and they never have known, and they don't want to be forced to learn.

Therefore, when every quality of care and patient safety expert is forced to agree that the current Healthcare Delivery System is broken, and when all of the evidence of the past several decades demonstrates that there is no evidence of real improvement in the quality of care and patient safety it should be time for dedicated activists to step forward.

Role Model:

MADD (Mothers Against Drunk Driving) has been my choice as a role model for my vision of what an organized group of activists might seek to emulate. MADD, here in South Carolina, have been successful in inducing the Legislature to take out the state's regulatory mechanism for drunk driving and attempt to close some of the existing loopholes in the laws.

After spending the past eight years attempting to convince multiple members of the Legislature, and former Governor Haley, without the slightest evidence of success, I have become convinced that a state-wide organization of concerned citizens who are fully informed of how the current system is, and has always been, flawed, and who also have an understanding of how to begin meaningful change in the current system can prove to be the deciding factor in finally making both the Governor and both houses of the Legislature get the message.

The ultimate goal in seeking to create a Healthcare Warrior organization would be to have a component of that organization in every community that has a hospital or surgery center, and in all other communities that desire to participate.

The Key Factor is finding the initial group of individuals who would step forward, and seek to rally like-mined individuals. I would not be the group's leader, or even a member, but I would dedicate myself to being their mentor, teacher, consultant, etc.

The first thing those initial activists need to be assured of is that I am fully able to provide them with the necessary guidance to rapidly become sufficiently knowledgeable enough to begin to challenge both the Governor and the Legislature. I believe there are numerous potential activists throughout this, and every other state, sufficient to create a formidable group that would be able to demand legislative consideration. They certainly couldn't make things worst.

This personal need to seek to entice a group of healthcare activists to become sufficiently organized to begin to make a difference is not a recent mental impulse. I came to this conclusion several years ago, and the longer it has germinated in my mind, the more convinced I have become that Healthcare Warriors can be the new factor that not only redirects all of the efforts to improve the quality of care and patent safety at the state level, but that movement can also be the device that forces the multiple Federal quality of care and patient safety agencies to finally be forced to recognize each state's responsibility to create and maintain an effective Healthcare Delivery System, and also to recognize that the current system is a non-system and has always been devoid of any systematic characteristics.

I am certain that there are many individuals in every state who have been looking for, and hoping for, a method that would allow them to not only become active in the efforts to improve the quality of care and patient safety, but also to be optimistic that this new tool can be highly effective. Therefore there are two initial factors necessary for the first group of Healthcare Warriors to become reality.

Initial Activists to take the Lead
Confidence that I can help them become effective

I hope my second and third books, Misdiagnosed, and Find The Black Box, plus my efforts for the past eight years in South Carolina can provide them with sufficient assurance that I am fully able to fulfill my responsibility to them. I can only hope that some day I will have an opportunity to stand before a large audience of healthcare activists who are eager to become Healthcare Warriors.

Ordinary people have an opportunity to become part of a movement that can result in meaningful change for every person in their state, and can leave a lasting legacy for their future loved ones.

Healthcare Warriors can be the gift that keeps on giving!

Why only three pages on How to become a Healthcare Warrior? I am trying not to over think the offer. Those individuals inclined to become Healthcare Warriors know who they are, and why they would like to have an opportunity to become involved with a sincere effort to make a difference. What they need most is assurance that I am a qualified resource available to them who can help them become effective, and I can do that.

So more about me: I am 84 and counting, and I am as fully engaged in life as I have ever been. I am into staying abreast of activities in the quality of care and patient safety arena at the national, state, and local level every day. I have challenged a room full of quality of care and patient safety experts at three Federal Agencies multiple times since 2014. I have an exercise routine every morning before breakfast to help me stay somewhat fit, and my physician assures me that I am very healthy, particularly for my age. But potential activists have a right to question my fitness to be able to fulfill my responsibilities to them, and I welcome that. Retirement is not an active word in my vocabulary. Throughout my adult life I have always needed a goal, and my past military and dental profession careers support that. Should I be successful in inspiring healthcare activists to become organized at their state level would be a dream come true for me.

The Bottom Line: The day a group of activists in any state allow me to stand before them and begin to layout step-by-step how they can rapidly become qualified to challenge their governor and state legislators will be the day when Healthcare Warriors begin to redirect all of the efforts to improve the quality of care and patient safety in America at both the national and state level. Hopefully that will be sufficient encouragement to begin to light several fires.

Note: I am registering to run as a candidate for the South Carolina Legislature in my House District, and I am challenging a friend and 6-term incumbent. It appears that he will have at least two opponents in this year's race for that seat, and that is highly unusual. This election year includes races for our next Governor, Congressman Trey Gowdy's Congressional seat, and every member of the South Carolina House of Representatives, plus other state positions. I have been trying for eight years to share my concerns and my expertise with former Governor Haley, the Upstate Legislative Delegation consisting of 7 state senators, and 15 house members, plus numerous other state legislators throughout the state without success. Therefore I have decided to try to join them. Of course, trying to unseat an incumbent is a daunting task, but Columbus took a chance, and I hope to have an opportunity to share my views publicly. The primary is in early June.

Like the various match-making programs offered on T.V., I am looking for those individuals who are motivated to make real change in their, and their loved one's Healthcare Delivery System. Let's get together and begin to make Healthcare history.

CHAPTER 2

Why become a Healthcare Warrior

"Even if you cured cancer you couldn't get it to the people because the medical system is broken".

"There is no question that our nation's healthcare system is broken".

Medical errors are the 3rd leading cause of deaths in the U.S. following only heart disease and cancer.

Every new estimate of needless hospital deaths has been greater than all previous estimates for the past 28 years.

Becoming a patient in any hospital in America is like shooting craps in Las Vegas, not everyone come out a winner.

How many reasons do rightfully concerned citizens need in order to recognize the urgent need for action? An army of experts have been promising great improvement in the quality of care and patient safety efforts for over 30 years, and the above quotes are in essence their report card of abject failure. More importantly, there are obvious reasons why all of their efforts have been ineffective, and have resulted in the above dismal list of failure.

I have lived in Greenville SC for 25 years, and I have written my three books using a great deal of observation and recognition regarding the obvious flaws at both the state and local levels, therefore

I will use events of the past few years that have, or have not, taken place in Greenville, and in Columbia, the state capitol. But readers need to understand that I believe the events, and non-events, I will describe here in South Carolina are highly similar to Healthcare Delivery System failures in every state capitol, and at every community fortunate enough to have a hospital. Greenville and Columbia should be taken as reflections of what can be found throughout our nation's Healthcare Delivery System.

Misdiagnosed, Why Current Healthcare Change is Malpractice was my second book written in 2010. I have read a lot of books regarding the Healthcare Delivery System and I believe *Misdiagnosed* is the first book to attempt to depict one state's Healthcare Delivery System by identifying its various components. And my sincere hope was that someone would read my book and decide, "An excellent subject but I can provide a better book." I say that because I think the need to recognize how each state has attempted to organize their Healthcare Delivery System is very important.

Greenville Health System (GHS) is the largest collection of acute care hospitals in South Carolina and that system contains slightly over 10% of the 65 hospitals in South Carolina today. GHS has two separate hospitals in Greenville, two hospitals in adjacent communities, and three rural hospitals in other counties, plus a Children's Hospital, a mental hospital, and a new medical school, plus additional facilities. In 2008 Gov. Sanford signed a bill expanding the GHS Board of Trustees from seven members to 12. Also in 2008 GHS and USC Medical School signed an agreement that created the USC/GHS Academic Health System, and the first class of students began in 2012.

A summary of events beginning in 2010, and currently continuing into the future is provided in an attempt to illustrate at both local and state level highly questionable events that have been taking place here in South Carolina, and in my opinion, a glimpse at how one state's failure to provide *lawful authority* over its entire Healthcare Delivery

System can perhaps be a harbinger of similar failings in most, if not all other states.

Dr. Spence Taylor, current GHS president said, *"Even if you cured cancer you couldn't get it to the people because the medical system is broken"* in the Greenville Journal in April 2010 while acting as the chairman of the committee creating the new GHS medical school. Dr. Taylor was not asked to elaborate on his candid comment, and he has never offered to publicly provide details regarding this critical assessment since. Furthermore, there is no evidence that Dr. Taylor, in his multiple meetings with various legislators and USC medical school officials offered details of his evaluation of the state's current healthcare delivery system to lawmakers in the state capitol.

Misdiagnosed was published in September 2010, and it contain the following blurb, *"This book is a call for state legislators around the country to fulfill their responsibility to restructure healthcare."* Bruce Bannister, SC House Assist. Majority Leader. At that time I lived in Representative Banister's House District and had met with him several times voicing my concern about the obvious problems within the current Healthcare Delivery System. In 2011 the House District lines were redrawn and I became a voter in Representative Garry Smith's House District. 2010 was also the year that Nikki Haley stunned the political pundits and was elected Governor of South Carolina.

In January 2011 I hand-delivered a packet to the Chairman of Gov. Haley's transition team here in Greenville with my offer to provide her and the state legislature with a detail depiction of the current Healthcare Delivery System. I have no knowledge if that packet was delivered to the Governor or if she gave its contents any consideration.

In April 2011 the Spartanburg Regional Hospital Pres./CEO and former president of the South Carolina Hospital Association said, *"There is no question that our nation's healthcare system is broken."* in an article he wrote for the Greenville Magazine.

In late August I had an opportunity to briefly meet face-to-face with Gov. Haley, and I shared with her both Dr. Taylor's and the Spartanburg Regional Hospital president's assessments of the current Healthcare Delivery System and again offered to provide her and the state legislature with a detailed depiction of that system. Gov. Haley had just published a book entitled *Can't Is Not An Option*, but her only response to my offer was, "I can't."

During the next several years I appeared before the Upstate Legislative Delegation several times and always shared with them those two quotes and my offer to provide the governor and state legislature with a detailed depiction of the current system to no avail. I also attempted to share my views with the Greenville News, the Greenville Journal, the Greenville and suburb Chambers of Commerce, various Tea Party groups, etc. and received absolutely no interest in their being provided with information regarding their and their loved ones Healthcare Delivery System. In April 2014 I was a Keynote Presenter at the 11th World Health Care Congress meeting across the Potomac from Washington DC, and I was probably the only speaker to speak about each state's responsibility and the fact that the current system was and had always been a non-system devoid of any systematic characteristic during that 3-day meeting with dozens of speakers.

In 2015 a majority of the GHS Board of Trustees voted to transfer ownership of the GHS Healthcare System from a public not-for-profit entity to a private non-profit entity. That is an over-simplification of what really happened. Did GHS break the law governing South Carolina hospital governance when a very small group of individuals, the majority in their GHS Board positions as unpaid volunteers, and who were expected to contribute only approximately 110 hours of board service and 5 days at retreats and conferences per year, and each was to be limited to two three-year terms, signed a presumed to be legal document transferring ownership to themselves? That question remains unanswered four years later.

Not only did 10 of the 12 current unpaid volunteer trustees sign the document that they assumed transferred ownership from the public to themselves, but shortly after that highly questionable event the board leadership proceeded to create two new boards, and triple the number of trustees on those three boards thereby rendering the original board to the status of a doormat.

While about half of the Upstate Legislative Delegation house members and one or two senators took great exception to the GHS transfer of ownership, most delegation senators and the other half of the house members remain silent, and the media coverage between the two camps became divisive and remains such. Thus the GHS leadership acted as though they were the authority of their domain, and the complete silence in response to that unilateral transaction from the governor's office and the state legislative leadership in Columbia appeared to support the understanding that South Carolina's government had never created any form of *lawful authority* over the current Healthcare Delivery System.

In early January 2016 my Representative Garry Smith nominated me to become a member of the GHS Board of Trustees and I was delighted. But at the Upstate Legislative Delegation meeting that month my nomination was blocked by a senator. However, several days later I was asked to meet with the GHS Nominating Committee as they were in the process of selecting over 20 new members for their new boards, and unfortunately I was not selected to become a member of one of those boards.

My possible nomination to the GHS Board of Trustees was again deferred at the Upstate Legislative Delegation meeting in April, and at their July meeting it was determined that I would not be selected for that board. My disappointment was great and I have to admit that I went into a mental funk for several days, and then I made the decision that it was time for me to attempt to share my views on why the current Healthcare Delivery System is broken, and has always been broken, and that I needed to begin to make more positive steps to accomplish that.

I soon discovered that the National Academy of Medicine (NAM) formerly the Institute of Medicine (IOM) was having an all-day meeting in Washington DC in late September on a Monday, and that the Agency for Healthcare Research and Quality (AHRQ) was having an all-day meeting two days later and I immediately registered for both meetings. I then prepared the following letters for the NAM and AHRQ Presidents.

Dr. Ira E. Williams
121 Lansfair Way
Greenville, SC 29607
864-676-1420
drirawilliams@gmail.com
www.findtheblackbox.org

September 26, 2016

Victor J. Dzau, President
National Academy of Medicine

Subject: The Two Greatest Healthcare Mistakes

Medical errors are now considered to be the 3rd leading cause of deaths in the U.S., and every new estimate of needless hospital deaths has been greater than all previous estimates for the past quarter century, and since Brennan & Leape (1990).

There are reasons why no discernable progress has been made in improving the quality of healthcare and patient safety, and I suggest that many of those reasons can be found in;

The Two Greatest Healthcare Mistakes that have been unrecognized or ignored.

I am requesting The National Academy of Medicine permit me to present;

- The Two Greatest Healthcare Mistakes
- A 3-step process on how to begin to create a 21st century healthcare delivery system.

In those presentations I will identify, and describe in detail what has always been missing in the efforts to improve the quality of healthcare and patient safety.

Semmelweis did not create the fact that IF doctors washed their hands, and sterilized their instruments fewer patients would needlessly die. He recognized, tested, and proved the life-saving value of those patient-care facts, but his patient-care advancements were not accepted by the medical leadership of his day.

I did not create the facts that support the understanding of the Two Greatest Healthcare Mistakes, and how recognition of those mistakes can provide the means to begin to create a 21st century healthcare delivery system. I can only hope that my request will not receive similar response as that received by Semmelweis, first in Vienna, and later in Budapest.

Experts should not only be challenged, but they should seek to be challenged.

Sincerely,
Ira E. Williams, D.D.S.

A similar letter was also hand-delivered to Dr. Bindman, then AHRQ President at that meeting two days later. Dr. Dzau has never responded to my letter to the National Academy of Medicine, but several weeks after returning home I did receive an email from the AHRQ Deputy Director suggesting that I write articles to journals regarding my concerns expressed in my letter. I replied by email that I had written three books on the subject and would be happy to discuss my views with them, but again I have received no further response.

While attending the National Academy of Medicine meeting I was able to meet with the highest healthcare officer in another state and shared with him my offer to Gov. Haley that I could provide a detailed picture of any state's current Healthcare Delivery System. This exchange led to my having an opportunity to travel to that state capital and layout my vision of how to create a detailed picture of any state's current Healthcare Delivery System, but sadly there was no positive response to my offer.

2017 was a very interesting year regarding my efforts to contribute to the efforts to improve the quality of care and patient safety both here in South Carolina and at the national level. In mid-July I traveled to Washington DC to attend an all-day meeting at the National Academy of Medicine, and the following are my notes I made after returning home. I also have a video record of that day's meeting, including my morning and afternoon questions.

National Academy of Medicine July 17, 2017: My comments at the meeting and my thoughts regarding the proceedings.

My comments during 1st morning session Q&A:
I have 3 Questions & 1 Recommendation:

1st – Since all medical care is local and states license doctors, and since all 50 state medical examining boards are each over 100 years old, and since each board has a mission statement containing the phrase, "to regulate practice of medicine", why aren't each state's responsibility to create and maintain an effective Healthcare Delivery System recognized?

2nd – Since To Err Is Human and Elizabeth McGlynn's Rand Corp. article both passively recognized that the "current system" is actually a "non-system", why has that critical recognition been consistently ignored?

3rd – Are Medical Errors the 3rd Leading Cause of Deaths, or are they the 5th, 7th, 9th, and does even one person know the truth?

Today's meeting is focused on 8 Goals & 20 Recommendations offered in Improving Diagnosis in Health Care published by the

National Academy of Medicine. How long would it take to make these 8 Goals & 20 Recommendations to become reality in any area's hospitals? Until these 8 Goals & 20 Recommendations can become reality in most hospitals they will remain merely words on paper. (My questions received NO response from the morning session panel)

After lunch I attended Break Out Group 3:
Patient-Centered Health Care, Education, and Policy to Improve Diagnosis:
 Pascale Carayon, Un. Wisconsin-Madison, and Kathryn McDonald, Stanford Un. were the Group moderators.

My comments regarding Goal 6 and its focus on the medical liability system:
 There are 3 systems with the potential to review questionable patient care and one of those systems, medical peer review is rarely ever mentioned, yet it is the only one of the three systems that is entirely controlled by doctors. Hospital medical staffs are the most important element in the healthcare delivery system, and their first priority is, or should be, to protect the public they serve from unqualified doctor-care.

3 Foundation Presidents attended that meeting:
 Harvey Fineberg, President, Gorden and Betty Moore Foundation
 Christopher Koller, President, Milbank Memorial Fund
 George Thibault, President, Josiah Macy Jr. Foundation.
 (Dr. Fineberg is the immediate past president of the National Academy of Medicine)
 I spoke with all three, and had a particularly detail conversation with Dr. Fineberg regarding each state's responsibility to create and maintain an effective Healthcare Delivery System. Nether he or any other of the Foundation Presidents showed any interest in that subject.

My comments at the mid-afternoon session Q&A:

I know it has been a long day, and everyone is tired, but I hope you each will respond to my two brief questions: Is the current "system" broken? It appeared that every person in the room raised their hand in affirmation. I then asked, Is the current system a non-system? Again, it appeared that every person in the room raised their hand in affirmation. I then said, Too many experts have been seeking for years for how to improve the quality of healthcare and patient safety in a non-system that has always been broken, and I don't understand that. The word "system" implies a tangible reality, and I do not believe we can ever create a 21st century Healthcare Delivery System without recognition of each state's responsibility and based upon a true system with an organizational structure.

I repeat, I have the entire video record of that meeting, including my comments, and also the fact that none of my questions or comments were ever responded to.

It should be noted that the National Academy of Medicine and AHRQ both continue in their efforts to improve the quality of care and patient safety while ignoring each state's responsibility to create and maintain an effective Healthcare Delivery System, and the long-recognized fact that the current "system" is, and has always been devoid of any systematic characteristics, but more on AHRQ later.

My brief tenure as a student in the Clemson University Graduate School Department of Public Health Sciences:

I contacted the Clemson Graduate School after hearing that South Carolina permits senior citizens to attend universities tuition-free, and I decided to see if I could possibly seek a masters degree in Health Sciences. I particularly wanted to compare my understanding of the current Healthcare Delivery System with what was being taught at that level. I wanted to courteously challenge and be challenged.

In mid-May I received an opportunity to visit the Clemson campus located about 40 miles West of Greenville, and meet with one of the Graduate School's professors. He was very informative, and we were fortunate to briefly meet with the Chairman of the Graduate Department of Public Health Sciences. The Chairman had come to Clemson from the Military Medical School in Bethesda MD, and knew members of AHRQ. He provided me with a brochure regarding a Graduate class that would begin in late August, and the classes would meet one night each week in Greenville. I was delighted, and began the process of enrolling.

There are two particulars regarding my enrollment process that are most memorable to me. I graduated from the University of Tennessee Dental School in Memphis in 1961, but Clemson required I provide them with a copy of my transcripts. Fortunately, the University was able to send copies of my transcripts to Clemson, and to this Golden Graduate (50 years) alum. Also, being technologically challenged I could have never successfully completed the enrollment process without the guidance and help from the Department Chairman's Administrative Assistant. She was an angel, though we had never met.

Classes began in August, and the class consisted of 8 students and me, and the students ranged from recent graduates, to two GHS doctors, and other hospital employees interested in acquiring the ability to participate in clinical research projects involving humans, animals, or devices. And while I enjoyed the classes, and educational stimulation, it became clear to me that there was no possibility for a person of my age to ever be able to participate in clinical research. I am very interested in doing medical research, but in areas involving hospital medical staffs, and regarding hospital medical staff issues that hospital medical staffs prefer not to investigate. Also, during the class weeks in September and October is the period when I was struggling with the decision regarding possibly challenging for the seat in my Legislative House District in the coming election process. Therefore, at the mid-term exam I offered my request to withdraw from the class. Plus, I had seen that University Graduate Schools do not teach their students anything about each state's responsibility to create and maintain an effective Healthcare Delivery System, and also that this thing everyone keeps calling a "system" is, and has always been devoid of any systematic characteristics. But interesting events for me in 2017 were not finished.

AHRQ has a National Advisory Council with about 15 members selected from across the nation, and AHRQ announced that they were accepting nominations, including self-nominations for 2018 since Advisory Council members serve three-year terms, and several members, including current Council Chairman Kaiser's Elizabeth McGlynn would be rotating off as Council members. I immediately submitted my self-nomination, and later obtained supporting letters from SC Senators Graham and Scott, and SC Lt. Gov. Bryant. As of mid-April, 2018 AHRQ has not published a list of new Council members.

I have attempted to describe, with brief comments, multiple fluid and on-going events regarding everyone's Healthcare Delivery System, and how decision-makers at the state government, and local levels, Federal Agencies, and Graduate University faculty function, while each of them claim their efforts are directed toward making the system better. And I hope I have been able to demonstrate that the current system is truly broken, and has always been broken, and that there is a desperate need for a well-organized group of activists to step forward and begin to demand meaningful change in every state.

Putting my money where my mouth is:

March 19, 2018 I registered my candidacy for SC House District 27, and I have been dividing my time between writing this book, and trying to organize a political campaign. I am challenging a friend, Garry Smith, who is a 6-term incumbent, not because I am against the way he has been voting in the Legislature, but because I can do something that neither he, or any other current Legislator can do. My mission, if elected, would be to begin a process to create a 21st century Healthcare Delivery System. I also believe that, if elected, the position of state legislator would be greatly beneficial to my effort to help any group of activists in any state to begin to create a Healthcare Warriors organization. In fact, one of the reasons I have elected to run for state office is to help me gain attention for my desire to help activists become aware that there is someone capable of helping them become effective in any effort to begin to make a difference in their state.

Healthcare Warriors can be the game-changer so desperately needed in the efforts to make our nation's Healthcare Delivery System finally begin to be transformed into a 21st century Healthcare Delivery System worthy of that label.

CHAPTER 3

One State's Current System

South Carolina's Healthcare Delivery System has been the model used in my previous books because I have lived here for the past quarter century, and I have not only studied that system intensely, but I have been a patient in that system several times, and survived to proclaim that while the current system is, and has always been broken, the vast majority of medical care is at least acceptable, and much of it is exceptional.

I believe the phrase, "don't throw the baby out with the bath water" is apt here. Our nation's Healthcare Delivery System is by far the best in the world, and even though our economic system has thwarted efforts to establish suitable methods for how to pay for care after-the-fact, the delivery of care far surpasses that of any other nation. Still the very nature of humans medically treating other humans demand that there be a constant effort seeking improvement in all aspects, and there is overwhelming evidence that much improvement in the quality of care and patient safety still must be achieved. And that understanding leads me to my seemingly solitary crusade; is each state responsible to create and maintain an effective Healthcare Delivery System? I will describe the South Carolina Healthcare Delivery System and let each reader be the judge.

South Carolina Healthcare Delivery System Components
State Agencies:
   Medical Examining Board
   DHEC
   DHHS – plus associated organizations:
   Medicare certification of hospitals:
   Joint Commission
   DNV-HC
   Medicaid certification companies:
   QIO
   QIO

Associations: Membership organizations.
   SC Medical Association
   SC Hospital Association

Medical Schools:
   SC Medical School (Columbia)
   Medical University of SC (Charleston)

Arnold School of Public Health
Moore School of Business
Health Sciences of SC
SC Governor's Quality Award (Baldrige)

     SC Medical Examining Board was created in the late 1880s, and its mission statement contains the phrase, "to regulate the practice of medicine", but no mention of that agency ever appears when highly questionable patient care events become newsworthy. In fact this state healthcare agency in rarely mentioned.
     Department of Health and Environmental Control (DHEC) was created sometime in the early 1950s, and at that time the combination might have made sense (perhaps), but DHEC has become the largest bureaucratic agency in the state, and I have hard evidence of several failures regarding their healthcare efforts. I personally

believe the Legislature should have taken advice from Solomon and divided this "baby" early in the 21^{s}t century.

Department of Health and Human Services is one of Lyndon Johnson's gifts that keeps on giving as a result of his disastrous Great Society. State HHS agencies are charged with the task of administrating Medicaid. Few people these days realize that when Congress was creating Medicare in the mid-1960s Medicaid was added as an after-thought with their thinking that this addition would never likely amount to much. Medicaid has been bleeding the states ever since.

Medicare and Medicaid's associated components were added, and periodically relabeled at the whim of the Centers for Medicare and Medicaid Services (CMS) headquartered in Baltimore MD, and each of the following components are tasked with certifying the quality of care provided by those hospitals, etc. eligible to receive funds from CMS. CMS claims the responsibility to certify the quality of care in hospitals, etc., while at the same time being forced to acknowledge that they have been losing in the neighborhood of $60B each year due to fraud. So much for Governmental oversight.

Joint Commission, DNV-Healthcare, and the American Osteopathic Association have received the CMS blessing to certify hospitals, etc. periodically as eligible to continue to receive Medicare payment for patient care. There have been numerous articles about the highly questionable certification process by the Joint Commission for decades, but nothing meaningful has ever changed regarding that dubious process. Ain't bureaucracies great?

Quality Improvement Organizations are spinoffs from PROs, PSROs, etc. since the original passage of Medicare/Medicaid, and they too were created to insure that quality of care was the norm in all hospitals, etc. receiving CMS payments. Yet CMS seems to ignore those experts who long have been saying, medical errors are the 3rd leading cause of deaths behind heart disease and cancer, and every new estimate of needless hospital deaths has been greater than all previous estimates for the past 28 years.

SC Medical Association (SCMA) and SC Hospital Association (SCHA) are membership associations, and as such always put their member's concerns before those of the public. Example, Dr. Spence Taylor was consulting with the SCHA, and state legislators when he said the medical system was broken in 2010, and Michael Riordan, then GHS Pres./CEO was a member of the SCHA Board of Trustees in 2011 when the Pres./CEO and former SCHA President said there was no question that the current system was broken. But there is no evidence that those three healthcare experts were urgently sharing their critical assessments with the Governor or Legislative Leadership. That major disconnect is conveniently ignored by everyone tasked with the responsibility to contribute to the efforts to make the quality of care and patient safety of the current system better.

Medical Schools: (as of 2010
    SC Medical School (Columbia)
    Medical University of SC (Charleston)

(As of 2016)
    USC/Greenville Medical School
    VCOM-Carolinas Osteopathic Medical School

Arnold School of Public Health is located in Columbia and is associated with the University of South Carolina. There are 40+ schools of public health, plus other associate schools, and there appears to be no recognition of state responsibility in those schools. My efforts to connect with faculty members at the Arnold School after writing Misdiagnosed in 2010 were met with disinterest.

Moore School of Business primarily deals with how-to-pay for healthcare after-the-fact, and contributes little if any consideration regarding the organizational structure of the Healthcare Delivery System.

Health Sciences of South Carolina is a public/private health organization established in 2004 by a collaboration between large hospital systems and medical schools with a focus on research.

SC Governor's Quality Award (Baldrige) The SC Quality Forum was established in 1991 to recognize and encourage improvements in quality and competitiveness by organizations throughout South Carolina, and uses the Baldrige Performance Excellence Program to accomplish this mission. But somehow the quality in healthcare doesn't seem to be improving.

So, there you have a snapshot of the various components of one state's Healthcare Delivery System, and my purpose in including it is to hopefully spur others to take a long hard look at their state's Healthcare Delivery System, while keeping in mind that the next time they or a loved one becomes a patient in one of their state's hospitals they will have more than merely a passing understanding of how that "system" might respond if that planned medical care becomes questionable.

I have performed major surgery on many patients, and I have been rolled into the operating room as a patient to undergo major surgery, and therefore I have first hand knowledge that the delivery of healthcare is a very personal event when you are on the receiving end. And that is why I am somewhat amazed that more people aren't demanding to know why there are so many questions regarding why the quality of care and patient safety continue to be so problematic. Well, as far as I am concerned, there are multiple reasons why care continues to be so problematic, and I am trying to share information about those reasons with as many people as possible.

Which brings me to a point of understanding that might interest those who do question why so little progress has been made to improve the quality of care and patient safety. Ask any person who claims expertise regarding the Healthcare Delivery SYSTEM IF they can describe in detail their state's Healthcare Delivery System.

I believe that not only should every person claiming expertise regarding the current Healthcare Delivery System be challenged, but that such persons should seek to be challenged. Sadly, I have found just the opposite reaction from every Healthcare Delivery System expert I have ever met, or sent a copy of my book Find The Black Box to, and each of the Federal Agencies created to improve the quality of care and patent safety. They know what they know, and don't confuse them with the facts.

I also believe that the first question that must be asked and answered in any attempt to begin to create a 21st century Healthcare Delivery System is;

Where are we now, and how did we get here?

Describing your state's current Healthcare Delivery System in detail, and identifying any presumed systematic characteristics is what is required to answer that critical question. Never try to change something you can't first describe in detail, and particularly something as enormous, complex, and critically important as Your and Your Loved Ones Healthcare Delivery System.

My Challenge to Potential Healthcare Activists

States are the key to all future efforts to begin to create a 21st century Healthcare Delivery System, and it appears that I am the only Healthcare Delivery System expert saying that. But I also say, prove me wrong.

Therefore, anyone who has a desire to make a meaningful difference, and leave something behind that will hopefully signify their existence, and who chooses their and their loved ones Healthcare Delivery System as their target, they must accept my belief that all states, and their state in particular, is where the action is most needed.

I have spent the past decade writing Misdiagnosed and Find The Black Box, and also challenging multiple Federal Agencies that were created to improve the quality of care and patient safety (with little success) and everything I see, hear, and read leaves me with only two conclusions:

States are responsible to create and maintain an effective Healthcare Delivery System.

Current "System" is, and has always been devoid of any systematic characteristics.

I am available to anyone interested in helping to form a Healthcare Warriors organization in their state, therefore I will use the remainder of this book to attempt to assure such persons of my past activities in staying abreast of efforts to improve the quality of care and patient safety at the national, state, and local levels while challenging experts at each of those levels, and illustrating many of the obvious flaws in those efforts during the past several decades, beginning with those Federal Agencies.

CHAPTER 4

The Bridge

The Bridge: I believe it is necessary at this point to create a *bridge* between the initial chapters, and what is to follow. Thus far I have attempted to provide two major points:

1. Why I am convinced that the current Healthcare Delivery System is "broken" because of the failure at every level to recognize each state's responsibility to create and maintain an effective Healthcare Delivery System.
2. Why Healthcare Warriors can, with my help, become highly effective activists in forcing their state Governor and Legislature to begin to make meaningful change in their state, and how such an activist movement in even one state could be the game-changer leading to efforts to begin to create a 21st century Healthcare Delivery System worthy of that label.

Others must determine if my offering is sufficiently credible enough to cause enough individuals to take-up my challenge and seek to participate in possible efforts to begin to organized like-minded people throughout their state, and response to this book will demonstrate the potential for Healthcare Warriors becoming reality.

The remaining chapters in this book will be my attempt to convince those so inclined that I;

- Have a deep understanding of the current Healthcare Delivery System.
- Have a proven track record of challenging quality of care and patient safety experts at every level regarding their failure to recognize each state's responsibility regarding the delivery of healthcare.
- Have the ability to share my expertise with dedicated activists sufficient for them to become effective forces for meaningful change where they and their loved ones live.

In essence, the initial chapters must be sufficient to cause multiple individuals to flip-the-switch and decide to become part of a major movement, and the later chapters are meant to reinforce their trust in a red-neck dentist who has spent most of his life challenging conventional wisdom. Together we can begin to create a whole new Healthcare World in America.

Also, my current campaign to become a member of the South Carolina House of Representatives will hopefully further assure interested individuals that I am serious. (This was written in 2018 prior to my failed campaign, as I had anticipated it would because I challenged my friend and Representative primarily to raise the issue of our State's broken Healthcare Delivery System, and I desired to publish this book in Ebook form only during the campaign.)

CHAPTER 5

How It All Began

Early Years – Birth & Cradle

People, when sufficiently sick or injured, seek the services of a doctor (or doctors) and a hospital; the basic unit of the Healthcare Delivery System, the largest, and most advanced such system in the world. Yet that enormous, complex system is a study in contrasts; the envy of the world in technical achievements, while simultaneously being outrageously expensive, and excessively harmful to far too many of the patients it seeks to serve. Example, every new estimate of needless hospital deaths (never events) has been greater than all previous estimates for the past quarter century, and none of the Quality of Healthcare and Patient Safety Army of experts can provide answers as to why those estimates continue to go in the wrong direction.

Three major entities, federal and state governments, and various components of Organized Medicine have dominated the process that has led to the current Healthcare Delivery System configuration. Sadly, more questions than answers will arise regarding how those three major entities failed to collaborate in the creation of one of the most important social contributors for the benefit of all citizens.

I not only enjoy studying history, I think the history of healthcare, and particularly the evolution of the medical profession is very important. The First Phase of my process for how to begin to create a 21st century Healthcare Delivery System is to answer the question,

Where are we now, and how did we get here? Meaning one should always begin any attempt to "change" a large, complex system by first describing in detail the current organizational structure of that system. Therefore I will begin with a rapid stroll through the highlights of the evolution of our nation's current Healthcare Delivery System.

Healthcare delivery, as we know it today began the first day a man stepped ashore and said, "I am a doctor, and I treat patients." We now know that unfortunately the odds are that that doctor probably did not have a medical degree from an established medical school somewhere on the other side of the Atlantic Ocean. But that sad realization was the norm during the period of early colonization of the New World, and well into the 19th Century. The history of the medical profession has been well documented multiple times, and therefore only cursory references to that specific history will be included as made necessary in depicting the evolution of the current Healthcare Delivery System. Needless to say, the practice of medicine took place throughout the colonies with little, if any regulatory control by the fragmented efforts of colonial governing bodies.

As the key cities, primarily those with major sea-faring ports (Baltimore, Boston, Charleston, New York, and even Philadelphia) began to enlarge their population they became magnets for doctors, both degreed and non-degreed. And one city in particular became the Cradle for what was to ultimately become the current Healthcare Delivery System.

The Story of the Creation of the Nation's First Hospital

Philadelphia Hospital was founded in 1751 by Dr. Thomas Bond and Benjamin Franklin "to care for the sick – poor and insane who were wandering the streets of Philadelphia." Philadelphia was the fastest growing city in the 13 colonies, boasting a population of 15,000 by 17 50; by 1776, a population of 40,000 residents made Philadelphia the second largest English-speaking city in the British Empire.

The idea for the hospital originated with Dr. Thomas Bond. A wealthy Quaker, Bond moved to Philadelphia as a young man. He traveled to London in 1738 to complete his medical education; afterward, Bond traveled through Europe, spending time at the famous French hospital, the Hotel-Dieu in Paris, where he became impressed with the continent's new hospital movement. Bond returned to Philadelphia a year later, and in 1741 he was appointed Port Inspector for Contagious Diseases. It was during this time that Bond began to formulate his idea for a hospital in Philadelphia.

Bond was a leading citizen in Philadelphia, belonging to such prominent organizations as the Library Company, American Philosophical Society (founding member), and the Academy of Philadelphia, which evolved into the University of Pennsylvania. About 1750, Bond "conceived the idea of establishing a hospital in Philadelphia for the reception and cure of poor sick persons." No hospitals existed in the 13 colonies, and when Bond approached Philadelphians for support they were not convinced the endeavor was necessary. Frequently, Bond was asked what Benjamin Franklin thought of the idea. Presenting his idea to his friend Franklin, it was immediately received with excitement. Franklin became a strong supporter and advocate for the hospital. It was Franklin's backing that convinced many others that Bond's proposed hospital was worthy of support.

The Pennsylvania Assembly received a petition on January 20, 1751 signed by 33 of Philadelphia's leading citizens. Noticeably absent from the signatures is Benjamin Franklin; Franklin printed the document, but did not sign it. Acknowledging that the Assembly had many charitable provisions for the poor already, but a small provincial hospital was also necessary. Within two weeks, a second reading occurred and a bill was presented and approved to establish a hospital "to care for the sick poor of the province and for the reception and care of lunatics."

Rural members of the Assembly were not convinced the hospital was necessary, primarily because they thought the hospital would only service those in the city. However, it was Franklin who saved the day again with a clever plan to counter that claim. Franklin proposed that he could prove the populace supported the hospital bill by agreeing to raise 2000 pounds from private citizens. If he was successful, Franklin proposed, the Assembly had to match the funds with an additional 2000 pounds. The Assembly agreed to Franklin's plan, thinking his task was impossible, but they were ready to receive "the credit of being charitable without the expense."

Franklin's fundraising effort was more than successful. The Assembly signed the bill and presented it to Lieutenant Governor James Hamilton for approval. After amending the bill several times, Hamilton signed it into law on May 11, 1751. Patients were first seen at temporary location on Market Street (then High Street) until patients were admitted in the newly erected facility on 8th Street in 1756.

Franklin recounted his involvement in the founding of the hospital in a 1754 publication, Some Account of the Pennsylvania Hospital, which was used as the first development report. So pleased was Franklin that he later stated: "I do not remember any of my political manoeuvres, the success of which gave me at the time more pleasure…"

Federal Government: The very young United States of America had just elected its second President Adams in 1797, and tensions between the states in favor of a strong federal government, and states that favored strong state's rights left no time for those supreme decision-makers to even think about contributing to the efforts to create a Healthcare Delivery System.

Colonial (State) Governments: Pennsylvania's Colonial Assembly recognized their responsibility by *authorizing* the establishment of the first hospital, and soon after, the first medical school. Philadelphia became the cradle for today's Healthcare Delivery System, but that infantile *system* was going to labor through two centuries of struggles before beginning to embrace the Dawn of Modern Medicine.

Organized Medicine: There was no such thing as Organized Medicine, and even the first thought of any attempt to organize a large group of strong-willed individuals would not take place until almost a century after the first hospital began to accept patients. Any effort to organize the menagerie of degreed, non-degreed, and quacks that represented the medical profession would have been like trying to herd cats. Merely reading about the history of the Philadelphia Hospital medical staff, and the faculty of the Pennsylvania Medical School throughout the remainder of the 18th Century will illustrate the hostility between even the most acclaimed physicians of those days, and such unprofessional behavior would long continue.

CHAPTER 6

1800 – 1900
Growing Pains

Population in the New World was increasing, and the major cities were rapidly growing both in size, and in their efforts to establish a Healthcare Delivery System. Hospitals and medical schools were springing up wherever a group of doctors could gather sufficient support.

One of the best and quickest ways to grasp the true nature of our nation's Healthcare Delivery System during its early years is to read *Dr. Mutter's Marvels,* Cristin O'Keefe Aptowicz, 2014. Dr. Thomas Mutter (1811-1859) became one of the exceptional doctors, surgeons, and teachers of medical students during his much too short life span. He lost both parents at age 7, and yet was able to overcome multiple obstacles while seeking his place in society, but seek it he did.

"Mutter's entry into the Philadelphia medical school community in the mid-1830s coincided with a period second to none in America's medical history and that time would be remembered for "rivalry marked with jealousy and unfairness" among the doctors. Medical lore and literature would record abundant evidence of the personal abuse and criticism that medical men of the day rained upon one another, and of the bitter acrimony that often characterized any public discussion of important questions, especially that of treatment."

Mutter graduated from Pennsylvania Medical School, and felt compelled to go to Paris, where his exposure to so many world-renown practitioners allowed him to formulate his methods for surgically treating severely deformed patients. Two patient care characteristics he did not choose to copy was how most doctors, not only in Paris, but very where else, ignored the consideration for acceptable hygiene regarding their hands, clothes, and instruments, and how almost every doctor treated their patients with contempt, and in every form of undignified manner. Mutter treated all of his patients with great dignity and patience, and used the utmost care in hygienic methods that went far beyond those commonly used throughout the medical profession of his day. Mutter's ambidextrous ability allowed him to perform major plastic surgery procedures on mutilated patients without the use of any anesthetic support, and with great success.

But there is far more to Mutter's story than just recounting his surgical, and patient care ability, as well as his exceptional teaching ability. The Philadelphia Hospital medical staff was dominated by doctors who sought to limit competition. Following Mutter's return to Philadelphia he struggled to establish a surgical practice, but Philadelphia would finally obtain the services of a second medical school and hospital.

"Several efforts to establish a second medical school were made in the 1810s and early 1820s, but all efforts to obtain a charter from the state legislature were unsuccessful. This would all change in 1824, when the irascible Dr. George McClellan's ongoing quarrels with the University of Pennsylvania Medical Department resulted in his leaving to found his own school: Jefferson Medical College."

In the 10 years following Jefferson's founding, the "period of accommodation" between the university and its new rival was marked by bitter, unrelenting public confrontations, often instigated and led by the two public faces of those medical schools: McClellan for Jefferson and Dr. William Gibson for the University of Pennsylvania. Both men were chairs of surgery at their respective colleges, and both men had legendary fiery tempers and sharp tongues."

Jefferson Medical Schools "Famous Faculty of 41" included Dr. Mutter as the chair of surgery. *Dr. Mutter's Marvels* is a must read for those seeking to understand the dynamic and continuous machinations that were taking place during the evolution of the Healthcare Delivery System in the pre-Civil War half of the 19th century. But events beginning just prior to 1850, some dramatic, and one not so, would set the practice of medicine on a far different course, and three of those events took place almost simultaneously.

Anesthesia

Dentist Horace Wells attempted to provide ether anesthesia for the removal of a young boy's tooth at Harvard Medical School before students and faculty in 1844, but the patient continuously screamed out in pain, and Wells' effort was considered a fraud. Unfortunately for Wells, the boy later would admit that he had felt no pain, but Wells' condemnation persisted. Dentist William Morton, in 1846, was able to successfully assist Dr. John Collins Warren in the surgical removal of a small tumor on the patient's neck in the same Harvard amphitheater that was the scene of Wells' false-failure.

But one of the most important aspects of the history of ether, and soon after, chloroform's ability to remove surgical pain for their patients, many, and possibly most surgeons refused to even consider using anesthesia for their surgeries. Dr. Mutter, on the other hand, had just completed writing a new book on how he performed his surgeries without anesthesia when he received the news of this new medical marvel. Mutter instantly adopted this method for painless surgeries, and never looked back. This episode of how so many doctors could vehemently reject, and make great effort to obstruct the acceptance of medical care advancements will prove to be a common theme throughout the history of the medical profession, and in some ways continues today.

Germ Theory

The process necessary to convince doctors that they were killing too many of their patients by transferring *germs* from their unwashed hands, and unclean instruments took several decades, and several contributors, but only three of the most prominent contributors will be included here.

Dr. Ignaz Semmelweis 1818–1865

Semmelweis was a Hungarian physician who was employed as an assistant to the professor of the maternity clinic at the Vienna General Hospital in Austria in 1847. During that year he noticed that a close friend of his had cut his finger while he was doing an autopsy, and that friend soon died of symptoms like that of puerperal fever.

That event caused Semmelweis to connect two disparate epidemiological facts: the death rate at his hospital of women who gave birth was 13 percent, and at a nearby hospital run by nuns acting as midwives their death rate was 2 percent. He also had observed that medical students were going from the anatomical dissection room to the delivery room without changing their outer garments or washing their hands.

These observations led Semmelweis to become a medical maverick. He began a study that first merely caused doctors to wash their hands in a chlorine solution when they left the anatomical dissection room. The mortality rate from puerperal fever rapidly dropped to 2 percent. However instead of reporting his success at a meeting, Semmelweis said nothing. Finally a friend published two papers on the method, but by that time Semmelweis had started washing medical instruments as well as their hands.

The hospital director felt his leadership had been criticized by Semmelweis' studies, and he was furious. He blocked Semmelweis' promotion and the situation continued to deteriorate. Viennese doctors turned on their Hungarian maverick. The medical leaders in Vienna said that IF they were to accept his findings and his methods, they would be forced to admit that they, and their now recognized outdated patient care methods were, and long had been, the cause of their much higher death rate. That they would never do, in spite of his overwhelming evidence in greater patient safety.

Facing rejection by his medical colleagues in Vienna, he returned to Budapest; and there he brought his methods to a far more primitive hospital. Those methods allowed him to cut the death rate by puerperal fever to less than 1 percent. He continued to expand his studies into the need for greater hygiene by physicians until finally, in 1861, he wrote a book on his methods. However the medical community in Budapest was no more receptive then his colleagues in Vienna had been. His book and his methods were given poor reviews, and his response unfortunately grew from anger into rage and frustration.

In 1865 he suffered a mental breakdown and friends committed him to a mental institution. There, he ended his brief forty-seven-year life by cutting his finger and within days he died of the very infection that had killed his friend previously and from what he'd saved thousands of mothers.

Louis Pasteur 1822-1895

Louis Pasteur did not set out to advance medical science and yet throughout his decades of experimental scientific achievements his work ultimately led to many branches of science and contributed to theoretical concepts and practical applications of modern science. He made possible treatments for rabies, and rickets, chicken cholera, and other diseases and aided in the development of the first vaccines. Past years work set the stage for modern biology and biochemistry, but perhaps his greatest achievement was to become the bridge between Semmelweis and Lister. *Louis Pasteur* by Rene DuBos 1976 recounts in great detail of the contributions this non-doctor made toward creating a modern Healthcare Delivery System.

Joseph Lister 1827 – 1912

The "Father of Antiseptic Surgery" gained the attention Semmelweis earned and deserved, but Lister always acknowledged that he had stood on the shoulders of a Hungarian doctor who had been vilified by the leadership of the profession he had so loved and sought to serve.

The collaborative efforts of Semmelweis, Pasteur, Lister, and others allowed the medical profession of the 19th century to begin to save more lives than they needlessly killed. But recognition of the life-saving value of that collaboration would take too many generations before being fully accepted. A detailed study of the historical timeline of the medical profession beginning in 1800 and coming forward recognizes the individuals such as these three, and in almost every case the medical leadership of their day vehemently attacked and rejected the offerings of those pioneers. Dr. Oliver Wendell Holmes, Sr. was making the same recommendations as Semmelweis regarding the benefits of hand and instrument hygiene here in America in 1843, and facing the same response of rejection and ridicule. Sadly, one of the greatest causes of patient harm, and needless deaths today is the continuing failure of caregivers, and not just doctors, to practice safe hygiene in every contact with patients. (More on that later)

The full details of Semmelweis, his contributions, and his complete rejection by his profession's leadership is not a story one can expect to hear at a medical presentation. Ignaz Semmelweis offered one of the most fundamental necessities of quality healthcare: doctors must wash their hands and instruments, but his offer was rejected by those in the position to determine its acceptance.

Dr. Semmelweis did not create the fact(s) that doctors, by washing their hands and instruments could save lives. He recognized the positive results in patient safety that nuns, a few blocks away, were achieving, tested his theory, and proved the patient safety value achievable. The stories of Anesthesia and Germ Theory are merely two examples of how the medical profession's leadership willfully obstructed significant advances throughout their history, and that unfortunate, but deeply ingrained characteristic continues.

Almost all of the historical timeline regarding the advancements brought about by recognition of the *germ theory* took place in Western Europe except for the efforts by Dr. Oliver Wendell Holmes here in America, and perhaps others at the time of Semmelweis' unsuccessful efforts. The history of how the germ theory, and hand, and instrument hygiene became acceptable medical practice in America appears to be shrouded in mystery, but would be interesting to discover.

> **All truth passes through three stages;**
> **First, it is ridiculed**
> **Second, it is violently opposed**
> **Finally, it is accepted as being self-evident.**
> **Schopenhauer**

State Medical Examining Boards

Governors and state legislators began to recognize their responsibility regarding the Healthcare Delivery System in their state late in the 19th century by realizing that doctors, regardless of their stated professional status, deserved some regulatory oversight.

The Early Development of Medical Licensing Laws in the United States, 1875-1900 by Ronald Hamowy, Department of History, University of Alberta, and presented at the Sixth Annual Libertarian Scholars Conference, Princeton University, October, 1978. Printed version appeared in the *Journal of Libertarian Studies* 3, no. 1 (1979). The following is taken from Appendix 1 of his article. (Appendix A)

According to Mr. Hamowy there were 45 states and 5 territories as of 1900, but there were 49 state/territory medical examining boards. Kentucky (1874) was the first state to create a medical examining board. One state, Kansas, and two territories, Alaska and Oklahoma, created their boards after 1900. Hawaii had a medical examining board 63 years prior to statehood, and Alaska 46 years prior to statehood. New Mexico Territory was divided into two states, Arizona and New Mexico in 1912 completing the 48 Continental States of America. Each state medical examining board has a mission statement containing the phrase, "to regulate the practice of medicine". The subject of the effectiveness of each state medical examining board must be left to another day.

South Carolina General Assembly created State Board of Health 1878

SC State Board of Health opened in 1879. The South Carolina Medical Association was designated as the State Board of Health with the responsibility of serving as the "sole adviser of the State in all questions involving the protection of the public health within its limits." The office of State Health Officer was created to lead the department in 1908.

American Medical Association

Dr. Nathan Smith Davis founded the American Medical Association in 1847 when he was just thirty years old. As a young doctor in western New York in 1844, Davis was elected to serve in the New York Medical Society, where he worked to improve medical education and licensure. A year after his election, Davis introduced a resolution endorsing the establishment of a national medical association to "elevate the standard of medical education in the United States." Though considered "impractical, if not utopian" by some, Davis and others led the establishment of the AMA in the following year, 1847.

AMA 1848 first recommended that state governments register births, marriage and deaths.

Summary

Federal Government: Presidents, and Congress had been far too busy with other matters, (Civil War, westward expansion, and the rising industrial movement, etc.) to consider their part in the creation of a Healthcare Delivery System, and that lapse should be understandable. The National Academy of Sciences (NSA) was founded on March 3, 1863, at the height of the Civil War, but the Institute of Medicine (now the National Academy of Medicine April 25, 2015) would be founded 107 years later in 1970. One must assume that Territorial Governments had been given authority to act in accordance with the states and create medical examining boards, but federal governmental deep involvement in the healthcare system would have to wait for another century.

State Governments: The Healthcare Delivery System was being created one city, and one state at a time. Hospitals were being established, doctors were becoming *organized*, and state governors and legislators were showing signs of the need for some degree of medical regulation, or so they thought.

Organized Medicine: The birth of Organized Medicine took place in 1847, followed soon after by the creation of local and state medical societies, with the desire to "elevate the standard of medical education in the Untied States." Over a century later it should be left to each reader to determine for themselves how well that desire has been fulfilled.

CHAPTER 7

1900 – 1950
Early Development of a System

Some of the various components of our current Healthcare Delivery System began to be developed in an attempt to bring order out of chaos. Hospitals and medical schools had been springing up throughout the states, and soon to be states, and many, if not most, of both left much to be desired. American Medical Association, and its state and local medical societies formed the nascent elements of what was to become Organized Medicine.

American Hospital Association: In September 1899, eight hospital superintendents met in Cleveland to discuss common concerns and interests. The result of this informal gathering was the establishment of the Association of Hospital Superintendents, an organization to facilitate discussion among hospital administrators. For approximately eight years, the Association served as a private club for hospital superintendents, excluding from membership assistant superintendents and others involved in running the hospital. In 1906, membership restrictions were changed to allow those executive officers next in authority below the superintendent to be associate members without vote, and the name was officially changed to the American Hospital Association. Personal membership remained the basis of the AHA until 1918 when the first institutional membership structure was adopted.

Goal: These changes in name and membership base were part of a broader evolution in the thinking and perspective of early 20th century hospital administrators. In 1899, the goal of the superintendents' organization was: To facilitate the interchange of ideas, comparing and contrasting methods of management, the discussion of hospital economics, the inspection of hospitals, suggestions of better plans for operating them, and such other matters as may affect the general interests of the membership.

In 1907, shortly after the name change, the goal was abbreviated to: The promotion of economy and efficiency in hospital management.

In 1917, the year prior to adopting institutional membership, the Association broadened its objective: To promote the welfare of the people so far as it may be done by the institution, care, and management of hospitals and dispensaries with efficiency and economy; to aid in procuring the cooperation of all organizations with aims and objectives similar to those of this Association; and in general, to do all things that may best promote hospital efficiency.

In subsequent years, the language in the mission has been modified to reflect the social and health care climate of the times. In 1937, for example, the object specifically called for development of hospital and outpatient services and emphasized professional education and scientific research. In 1951, the object was again changed to strengthen the Association's commitment to development of better hospital care for all the people. Published with permission.

American College of Surgeons: ACS was established in Chicago IL, in 1913 at the initiative of Franklin Martin, M.D., FACS. The College is a surgical society dedicated to promoting the highest standards of surgical care through education of, and advocacy for, it's Fellows and their patients, and to safeguarding standards of care in an optimal and ethical practice environment.

The College was an outgrowth of the highly successful Clinical Congresses of Surgeons of North America, which took place annually from 1910 in various large surgical centers throughout North America as a means for continuing education of practicing surgeons. The

Clinical Congresses were, themselves, an outgrowth of the journal Surgery, Gynecology and Obstetrics, another initiative of ACS Founder Franklin H Martin. SG&O began publishing in 1905 as a vehicle for practicing surgeons to edit their own journal, unlike most other scientific medical journals of the day, with the exception of the Journal of the American Medical Association, which were published by non-medical commercial firms for profit. From the time of its origin, the College has been involved in surgical education and research, patient welfare, hospital standardization, ethics of practice, in collaboration with other medical associations. Courtesy of the American College of Surgeons Archives.

American College of Physicians: ACP is a national organization of internists – specialists who apply scientific knowledge and clinical expertise to the diagnosis, treatment, and compassionate care of adults across the spectrum from health to complex illness. The ACP mission is to enhance the quality and effectiveness of health care by fostering excellence and professionalism in the practice of medicine. ACP was founded in 1915 to promote the science and practice of medicine, and since 1915 has supported internists in their quest for excellence. By sharing the most updated medical knowledge, offering top-notch educational resources, and a wide array of additional benefits, ACP has shown a commitment to internal medicine and those who practice it.

Much has transpired in internal medicine and in healthcare over the last 100 years. ACP has changed as well and stands proudly as the largest medical specialty organization in the United States and a major voice in American health care. ACP's membership of 143,000 includes internists, internal medicine subspecialties, medical students, residents, and fellows, and a growing international presence. As ACP celebrates its centennial, the first 100 years of the College provide an inspiration for us all as ACP applies the rigorous scientific standards of internal medicine as the foundation for meeting the challenges ahead and for best serving our physicians and their patients.

State Medical Examining Boards

The last of the 50 state medical examining boards was created when the New Mexico Territory was divide into the states of Arizona and New Mexico, and Arizona created its own board. But what was happening in medical education?

Federation of State Medical Boards 1912 is established accepting AMA's rating of medical schools as authoritative.

Carnegie Foundation: Founded in 1905 and chartered in 1906 by an act of Congress, the Carnegie Foundation for the Advancement of Teaching has a long and distinguished history. It is an independent policy and research center, whose primary activities of research and writing have resulted in published reports on every level of education.

Flexner Report 2010

Carnegie Foundation commissioned Abraham Flexner to survey the quality of the 155 medical colleges in the U.S. and Canada in 1908. But how could Abraham Flexner, the middle son of nine children born to struggling German-Jewish immigrants in Louisville, Kentucky have dramatically improved medical education here and throughout the world with only two years of college and no medical experience? Timing was everything.

Early in the 20th century, medical education was in almost total disarray, with quality schools being the exception, rather than the norm. Flexner thus stood at the vortex of swiftly moving scientific, educational and philanthropic currents that strongly favored reform. Notice that there is no mention of government involvement in this ongoing process. Federal governmental participation in either the form of financial support or regulation was seemingly non-existent.

In Flexner's day, more than 150 schools, enrolling some 25,000 students, dotted the landscape across the United States and Canada. They were the survivors of some 457 medical schools that had sprung up willy-nilly in North America over the preceding century and a half. Approximately twice as many students were enrolled in those schools 1910 as had been 10 years earlier. Nearly half of the world's medical students, in fact, were crowded into American schools. A dozen universities offered quality instruction, and another 20 stood out from the rest.

Over the course of two years Flexner judged two thirds of the schools he visited to be utterly hopeless. For example some schools were found to have only one dust-covered microscope. 89 of the nation's schools, about 60% of the total, required for admission only the rudiments or the recollection of an elementary education. The litmus test was, "If the male student's father could pay the tuition the student was admitted.

The study was divided into two parts. The first would describe the historical evolution of medical teaching in America and lay down the minimum requirements for study, equipment, and finances in a modern school of medicine. The second part of the report would survey each medical school in the United States and Canada with a view to rooting out those with weak or inadequate programs.

Flexner's dramatic change in medical education can hardly be described as rapid. This report was presented in 1910 and Flexner spent the next 18 years implementing the goal to vastly improve medical education in America, as well as performing a similar study of medical education in Europe. The last unqualified medical schools were not eliminated until the early 1930s, proving there is no "magic wand" when fundamental change is indicated and required.

Flexner repeated the process several years later in Germany, France, England and the Low Countries. The results were phenomenal. On a visit to Berlin in 1928 he was awarded an honorary degree in medicine, the first ever awarded to a layperson. According to the Dean, "no discussion of medical education now takes place that does not start from the exposition of your views; no one else has ever treated the subject with such thoroughness, objectivity and comprehensiveness." 50 years later, a British medical Dean gave him credit for the present evolution of British medical education.

In 1956 at age 90, he was credited with having made the greatest single contribution that had ever been made to the advancement of medical education in America. After 100 years it is still the best known of all such surveys. Flexner was given credit for eliminating more bad schools in less time than in any other time in the history of the world.

America owes to Flexner, more than any other person, the rapid implementation of the full-time medical school, allied to a teaching hospital, and integrated into a university. It was he who defined what a medical school should and should not be. Flexner went on to establish the Institute for Advanced Study at Princeton in 1930, and he was instrumental in convincing Albert Einstein to come to America rather than go to England in 1933.

Iconoclast, Abraham Flexner and A Life in Learning, Thomas Neville, Bonner, The Johns Hopkins University Press. 2002.

Flexner Report is, or should be, the role model used to illustrate the great need to describe in detail the current Healthcare Delivery System, and initiate similar change in how each state's current system can hopefully be transformed.

American College of Surgeons began reviewing hospitals across the nation, and their findings were somewhat similar to what Flexner had been finding in his review of medical schools. There was much to be desired in both critical aspects of the nation's budding Healthcare Delivery System.

Organized Medicine as few have seen it

Organized medicine was represented solely by the founding of the American Medical Association (AMA) in 1847, followed by the American College of Surgeons (ACS) in 1913, and the American College of Physicians (ACP) in 1915.

Paul Starr best described the true measure of how doctors dominated healthcare in America throughout most of its history in America in his 1981 Pulitzer Prize winning book, *The Social Transformation of American Medicine.*

"Yet the replacement of a competitive orientation with a corporate consciousness required more than common interests. It required a transfer of power to the group, and this was what began to happen in medicine around 1900 with changes in its social structure. Physicians came increasingly to rely on each other's good will for their access to patients and facilities. Physicians also depended more on their colleagues for defense against malpractice suits, which were increasing in frequency. The courts, in working out the rules of liability for medical practice in the late nineteenth century, had set as the standard of care that of the local community where the physicians practiced.

This limited possible expert testimony against physicians to their immediate colleagues. By adopting the "locality rule," the courts prepared the way for granting considerable power to the local medical society, for it became almost impossible for patients to get testimony against a physician who was a member. Medical societies began to make malpractice defense a direct service. Shortly after the turn of the century, doctors in New York, Chicago, and Cleveland organized common defense funds. The Massachusetts Medical Society began handling malpractice suits in 1908. During the next ten years, it supported accused physicians in all but three of the ninety-four cases it received. Only twelve of these ninety-one cases went to trial, all save one resulting in a victory for the doctor. For its first twenty years, the defense fund of the medical society of the state of Washington won every case it fought. Because of their ability to protect their members, medical societies were able to get low insurance rates, while doctors who did not belong could scarcely get any insurance protection. This provided the sort of "selected incentive" that medical societies needed to help them attract members. Professional ostracism carried increasingly serious consequences: denial of hospital privileges, loss of referrals, loss of malpractice insurance, and in extreme cases, loss of a license to practice. The local medical fraternity became the arbiter of a doctor's position and fortune, and he could no longer choose to ignore it. By making the county societies the gate-keeper to membership in any higher professional group, the AMA had recognized and strengthened the position of the local fraternity, as well as bolstering its own organizational underpinnings."

I considered Professor Starr's description of how the AMA controlled the practice of medicine in America 100 years ago similar to the way Al Capone controlled Chicago, the home of the AMA headquarters, for several years, through outright terror.

A department head at the Arnold School of Public Health at the University of South Carolina in Columbia, SC, told me that Professor Starr's book is still required reading at their institution more than thirty years after it was published. Both AMA and Arnold School of Public Health reinforce the understanding that old habits are hard to change.

Harvard School of Public Health: Founded: in 1913, grew out of the Harvard-MIT School for Health Officers, the nation's first graduate training program in public health

Johns Hopkins School of Hygiene and Public Health: Founded in 1916 as the first independent, degree-granting institution for research and training in public health, Johns Hopkins School of Public Health web site

Summary

Federal Government:
There were nine Presidents between 1900 and 1950 and they were forced to contend with major national events (WW I, stock market crash, Great Depression, WW II), and the Korean War began in June 1950 so it should not be surprising that creation of a Healthcare Delivery System by the federal government did not become a major priority during that half century.

State Governments:
South Carolina General Assembly created State Board of Health 1878
SC State Board of Health opened in 1879, and the office of State Health Officer was created to lead the department in 1908. And all 50

states or future states had created medical examining boards by 1912. South Carolina will serve as the state example of efforts at that level of government because any attempt to record the convoluted efforts in all 50 states would be beyond the scope of this book. Hopefully others will examine the evolution of the Healthcare Delivery System in their state for comparison.

Organized Medicine:

Organized Medicine had firmly established a solid foundation when the AMA was joined by the ACS, and ACP, and with the AHA, each of them were promising higher standards, and ethical practitioner conduct, while Paul Starr describes a starkly contrasting picture. Doctors basically owned the Healthcare Delivery System for the first 80% of the history of that *system* thus far, and in many respects they treated it like a "good old boy's club." Criticism of this appraisal will hopefully be based upon facts.

Flexner Report had established the foundation for a far more modern medical education system, but fulfillment of that task would require several decades, and the last of the inferior medical schools were not eliminated until well into the 1930s. However, schools of Public Health were being founded and some recognition of the need to establish some form of organizational structure for the delivery of healthcare was beginning to take shape.

CHAPTER 8

Dawn of Modern Medicine

1950 – mid 1980

Official sunrise each day follows dawn's early light, and the period between the end of WW II in 1945, and January 1, 1950 might be considered the Dawn of Modern Medicine. Far more mature men and women were returning from the battle fields seeking more out of life, and the GI Bill opened futures through higher education that few of them could have previously imagined.

The GI Bill accelerated the rapid expansion in the fields of law, engineering, and medicine. Teaching hospitals were built and existing ones expanded, and medical specialization began to explode. Doctors who had served in field hospitals near the front lines, and those at more established facilities received training that far surpassed any thing they might have gained back home.

Arbitrarily one might consider January 1, 1950 the official sunrise of Modern Medicine because the Healthcare Delivery System was rapidly entering a new era at break-neck speed. The next 65 years (1950 – 2015) are by far the most significant period of evolution of the current Healthcare Delivery System, and that evolutionary process requires that period to be imprecisely divided into two halves (1950 – mid-1980s) and the remainder. The slow, but constantly enlarging growth of an army of Quality of Healthcare and Patient Safety experts during the second half of that bifurcated period is where a deep understanding of the need for a precise depiction of the current Healthcare Delivery System becomes so vital.

The Greatest Mistake in Healthcare has taken place beginning after January 1, 1950 and continuing today. While the federal government, and all state governments will be creating healthcare agencies, and Organized Medicine will become deeply involved in the federal government's efforts to expand the Cost & Access (how to pay for healthcare after-the-fact) aspect of healthcare a fundamental priority of all *systems* will be ignored. The nation that has allowed men to walk on the moon and return safely has never created an organizational structure for that enormous, complex *system* everyone, sooner or later, tries to talk about, and need.

The first half of the period between 1950 and present day was focused primarily on the Big Three (federal, states, and Organized Medicine) being the principle sources of components that were contributing to what was becoming the current Healthcare Delivery System. But beginning in the mid-1980s, and continuing today, a wide assortment of associations, foundations, think tanks, schools of public health, etc., and most particularly, Federal Agencies, have joined the efforts to improve the quality of healthcare and patient safety.

AMA Journal (JAMA) 1958

What marks a profession? It is obligated to assure the public of the competence of its members and the quality of their work. It is obligated to assume the responsibility of disciplining those who do not measure up to the accepted ethical practices of the profession. Only physicians can judge the competence of their colleagues and can prohibit the kinds of conduct harmful to patients and the profession. (That sounds too good to be true, doesn't it, and unfortunately it has been too good to be true.)

United States Department of Health, Education, and Welfare (HEW) was a cabinet-level department from 1953 until 1979. In

1979, a separate Department of Education was created, and HEW was renamed the **Department of Health and Human Services (HHS).**

Joint Commission

American Medical Association (AMA), American College of Surgeons (ACS), American College of Physicians (ACP), and American Hospital Association (AHA) jointly created the Joint Commission (JC) in 1951, but the importance of the JC would begin in 1965, and an assessment of their contribution to patient safety would depend upon who was asked, but much more will be offered regarding the JC later.

Federal Government

1965 President Johnson and Congress created Medicare and Medicaid. And the Joint Commission was *deemed* (a contractual agreement with little oversight) to *certify* hospitals eligible to receive Medicare reimbursements. [**Deeming resolution** is a term that refers to legislation deemed to serve as an annual budget resolution for purposes of establishing enforceable budget levels for a budget cycle. A deeming resolution is used when the House and Senate are late in reaching final agreement on a budget resolution are fail to reach agreement altogether. The term deeming resolution is not officially defined, nor is there any specific statue or rule authorizing such legislation. Instead, the use of a deeming resolution simply represents the House and Senate employing regular legislative procedures to deal with the issue on an ad hoc basis.]

England had socialized their healthcare system into the National Health Service in the late 1940s after the end of WW II, and consideration for major federal involvement in the delivery of healthcare and how such services were paid for became strongly divisive issues between governmental proponents of such considerations and Organized Medicine. The threat of *Socialized Medicine* became a rallying cry within the medical and dental professions throughout the nation years before President Johnson's Great Society.

1970 Institute of Medicine became a component of the **National Academy of Science**, and the first Federal quality of care and patient safety agency, with more to follow.

1979 President Carter and Congress separated Department of Health, Education, and Welfare by forming the Department of Education, and Department of Health and Human Services (DHHS) in 1980.

State Governments

All 50 states had long had state medical examining boards, each with a mission statement containing the phrase "to regulate the practice of medicine". Each state was also required to create agencies typically called DHHS to coordinate Medicaid patient services. Also each state would presumably create an agency to regulate the construction, and expansion of both physical, and patient care services.

Robert Wood Johnsons Foundation: Since 1972, we have worked to identify the most pressing health issues facing America. We believe that good health and health care are essential to the well-being and stability of our society and the vitality of our families and communities. Our work is guided by a fundamental premise: we are stewards of private funds that must be used in the public's interests. Together with our grantees and collaborators, we strive to bring about meaningful, lasting change – with a goal of building a Culture of Health that enables all in our diverse society to lead healthier lives, now and for generations to come.

John D. and Catherine T. MacArthur Foundation: Established in 1970, the Foundation began to award grants in 1979. The Foundation supports creative people and effective institutions committed to building a more just, verdant, and peaceful world. In addition to selecting the MacArthur Fellows, the Foundation works to defend human rights, advance global conservation and security, make cities better places, and understand how technology is affecting children and society.

Quality of Healthcare

Avedis Donabedian, MMD, MPH, Father of Quality Assurance (1919-2000)

How did an Armenian child born in Beirut, Lebanon due to the Armenian holocaust and just after the end of WW I become the Father of Quality Assurance in America? Serendipity appears to be the convoluted path followed by this person who dedicated his life to trying to quantify the quality of healthcare.

Donabedican, like his father, became a physician by obtaining his MD at the American University of Beirut in 1944. He served as a general practitioner physician in Jerusalem until 1954 when he moved to Boston. In 1955 he graduated from the Harvard School of Public Health with an MPH degree, and then taught preventive medicine at the New York Medical College from 1957 to 1961. The School of Public Health at the University of Michigan recruited him in 1961, and he remained there for 28 years. He retired in 1989 but continued to serve as emeritus professor until his death in November 2000.

He was the author of eight books, over 50 peer-reviewed articles and countless lectures and is considered the person who transformed thinking about health systems. As a result of his work, the field of health systems research has become a robust space for inquiry and an exciting arena for action, within which Donabedian focused his attention on the quality of healthcare.

Evaluating the quality of medical care, Donabedian, Milbank Memorial Fund quarterly, 1966 introduced the concepts of structure, process and outcome, which remain to our day as the dominant paradigm for the evaluation of the quality of healthcare.

Donabedian was very deeply involved in the passage of Medicare. The Institute of Medicine was a little group of 10 or 12 its first year in 1970, but the first time it opened up in 1971 to a large group Donabedian became a member with the first 300 inductees. A testimony to his influence is the existence of the Avedis Donabedian Foundation for the Improvement of Health Care in Barcelona Spain and several awards bearing his name. The quest seeking to quantify and improve the quality of healthcare was evolving just as the Federal Government was making its initial venture into how to pay for healthcare after-the-fact through Medicare and Medicaid.

Professional Standards Review Organizations (PSRO)

The 1972 Social Security amendments contain the landmark Professional Standards Review Organization (PSRO) provisions as well as several sections upgrading existing utilization review (UR) requirements under Medicare and Medicaid. With issuance of the PSRO Program Manual and the recent publication of the new UR regulations, HEW for the first time has brought Medicare and Medicaid hospital review requirements into conformity and made them compatible with and supportive of the PSRO program.

The Professional Standards Review Organization (PSRO) program was enacted on October 30, 1972 as part of the 1972 amendments to the Social Security Act. On March 15, 1974, the Department of Health, Education, and Welfare (DHEW) issued the first portion of the PSRO Program Manual. The Manual indicates that although PSROs are responsible for review of all institutional services, they are to give priority to the review of hospital care.

Peer Review Organization (PRO) replaced Professional Standards Review Organizations (PSRO) in 1984. PRO purpose was to provide State medical boards with information about physicians responsible for substandard medical care.

California Medical Injury Compensation Reform Act – 1975 (MICRA-75) set the cap for medical harm to patients at $250,000 and that cap remains at that level as of 2018. AMA recognized MICRA-75 as the "Gold Standard" for medical malpractice tort reform in 2003. California legislators don't seem to understand that $250,000 in 1975 is not the same as $250,000 in 2018, but California legislators seem to march to a different drummer.

Medical Malpractice Crisis

The initial wave of the medical malpractice crisis first took place in the early to mid-1970s, and its unexpected ramifications ripped through the entire medical and dental professions, even though an AMA/AHA joint committee had foreseen the potential for such an event in the late 1950s, but remained silent. And like a tsunami, the nation-wide medical malpractice crisis would wash across the nation for the next several decades. Patients were being medically harmed, and/or needlessly dying in hospitals and no one could identify the root cause or contribute to stemming that deadly tide.

The Quality of Healthcare and Patient Safety Army of experts would begin to evolve in the mid-1980s, heralded by a major patient safety undertaking. The primary focus, both in Congress, and state legislatures will begin to be on how to pay for healthcare after-the-fact (Cost & Access), an exceedingly important aspect of the Healthcare System as a whole. But all healthcare begins at the basic unit of that public service, the doctor/patient interface collectively known as the Healthcare Delivery System, and that hugely imbalanced focus primarily on the Cost & Access aspect of the Healthcare System as a whole has been accelerated throughout the past several decades. Both the Cost & Access aspect and the Healthcare Delivery System aspect are equally important, but unequally considered.

The Greatest Healthcare Mistake is the complete failure of creating a true Healthcare Delivery System comprised of an organizational structure with clearly defined points of authority, and delegated authority necessary for effective accountability. The nation that allowed men to walk on the moon and return safety has never created, attempted to create, or even thought about creating such a true *system*,

Accountability is a By-Product of Authority or Delegated Authority sufficient to be Effective

Authority and Delegated Authority can only exist in an effective manner when positioned in an established Organizational Structure

Organizational Structure with clearly defined points of Authority & Delegated Authority is what has always been missing in the current Healthcare Delivery System.

The key to **The Greatest Healthcare Mistake** is best demonstrated by an arduous attempt to describe in great detail what has now become since the mid-1980s the Quality of Healthcare and Patient Safety Army of experts. Additional congressionally created, and at least initially federally funded Quality of Healthcare and Patient Safety agencies have joined an enormous array of other organizations focused on the same target during the past four decades.

Since all medical care is local, and each state license doctors to practice medicine, each state should be responsible to create, and maintain an effective Healthcare Delivery System. Sadly, no state governor or state legislature, past or present, has ever fully recognized that grave responsibility. But any attempt to illustrate the multiple healthcare delivery agencies, and their systematic characteristics in all 50 states would be unmanageable in this type depiction, so demonstration of one state's current Healthcare Delivery System will be offered to hopefully be an acceptable example.

The Professions Under Siege,
Jacques Barzun, Harper's Magazine, October 1978

A profession is an institution, and as such it cuts a figure in public that may or may not match the prevailing habits and merits of the practitioners. The insiders genuinely believe in that figure; they live by it in more ways than one, and they can hardly help thinking of the profession as going on forever in the same glorious way, altering itself only as it improves performance by new skill.

According to Dr. Abraham Flexner, the famous critic and reformer of medical education 50 years ago, to be medically trained implies the possession of certain portions of many sciences arranged and organized with a distinct practical purpose in view. That is what makes it a profession. The key words here are: a distinct practical purpose in view, for which special training is required. Since the laity, by definition, has no such purposes and lack special training, a profession is necessarily a monopoly. In modern societies, this monopoly is made legal by license to practice; but the professions have always managed to form a guild, a trade union, claiming the exclusive right to practice the art. But between monopoly and conspiracy the line of demarcation is hard to fix and easy to step over.

What every professional should bear in mind is the distinction between a profession and a function. The function may well be the eternal; but the profession, which is a cluster of practices and relationships arising from the function at a given time and place, can be destroyed-or can destroy itself-very rapidly.

The modern professions have enjoyed their monopoly for so long that they have forgotten that it is a privilege given in exchange for a public benefit.

But what the professions need in their present predicament is, first, the will to police themselves with no fraternal hand, with no thought of public relations. Any few scandals giving the group a bad name will soon convince the public that self-policing means what it says and confidence will return. Screening and disciplining from within must always continue, steadily and firm, or will be taken over by public bodies and officialdom.

English has borrowed from French the phrase *esprit de corps* and uses it to mean something good – team spirit, loyalty. But in French, to this day, it means something bad: the huddling together of members of the guild to hush up their mistakes; it means in short, Shaw's conspiracy against the laity. (Bernard Shaw said, "Every profession is a conspiracy against the laity.")

Policing, being negative, is not enough. It will not affect moral regeneration, which can come about only when the members of a group feel once more confident that ethical behavior is desirable, widely practiced, approved, and admired.

What all professions need today is critics from inside, men who know what the conditions are, and also the arguments and excuses, and in a full sweep over the field can offer their fellow practitioners a new vision of the profession as an institution.

Summary

President Johnson and Congress discovered the power of the healthcare purse, and also began to try to improve the quality of care through the efforts of federal agencies.

States were building hospitals, and medical schools, and teaching hospitals at a rapid pace, and creating healthcare agencies, but without any recognition of the need for at least some semblance of organizational structure (system).

Organized Medicine was being expanded by multiple specialties, and their associations.

Quality of Healthcare and Patient Safety Army of experts began its transformation into becoming the fourth source capable of impacting the Healthcare Delivery System. This army of experts has become the fourth major component that directly impacts every effort to improve the quality of care and patient safety, and these are the experts who have refused to recognize each state's responsibility to create and maintain an effective Healthcare Delivery System. And they also recognized, but continue to ignore, the obvious fact that this thing that everyone is compelled to call a *system*, is devoid of any systematic characteristics, and the importance of that critical understanding. The word *system* implies multiple components functioning in unison with each other, and with a unified goal. Our nation and each state's current Healthcare Delivery System components function as if they each speak a different language, yet try to talk about any aspect of Healthcare and not be compelled to use the word *system* multiple times.

CHAPTER 9

Quality of Care Army of Experts

Mid-1980s – Present

The Healthcare Delivery System is a convenient label given to the collective patient-care services of all practicing physicians, and all hospital medical staffs at any given point in time. Unfortunately throughout the hundreds of years between the first day a doctor stepped ashore and the mid-1980s that *system* had always been devoid of any systematic characteristics while being dominated throughout that evolutionary period by three major sources; federal (colonial) and state governments, and the enlarging elements of Organized Medicine. But recognition of the need to try to *measure* the quality of healthcare that *system* provided patients began after the Dawn of Modern Medicine as demonstrated by Medicare, Medicaid, Joint Commission certification for Medicare payments to hospitals, PSROs, (later becoming PROs), and as illustrated by the early efforts of Dr. Donabedian, and others.

The Quality of Healthcare and Patient Safety Army of experts began to break out of its embryonic shell and begin its maturation process that has led it to becoming a fourth force joining the original Big Three in helping to shape the constantly evolving Healthcare Delivery system.

It is impossible to consider, and hope to better understand, the Healthcare Delivery System without seeking to describe how each of those four sources have contributed, each in their own way, leading to that *system's* current configuration. Those who have little, if any, awareness and understanding of the Quality of Healthcare and Patient Safety Army of experts should be shocked by its enormous size, complexity, and implied impact on how patient care has been provided during the past several decades, and assumed to be provided well into the future.

I choose 1986 as the pivotal point in how to include this fourth important source of major contributions to the evolutionary process of how the current Healthcare Delivery System has evolved into its present configuration due to three unrelated, and distinctly different seminal events that were first recorded for one, first began for another, and the third due to action by Congress during that year. The historical time line of the Healthcare Delivery System will take a dramatic redirection with the inclusion of this fourth major component.

1986

First event:
"Standards for Patient Monitoring During Anesthesia at Harvard Medical School" by John H. Eichhorn, MD; Jeffery B. Cooper, PhD; David J. Cullen, MD; Ward R. Maier, MD; James H. Philip, MD; Robert G. Seeman, MD; JAMA, August 22, 1986.

Harvard is self-insured and has its own risk management organization. Even so, Harvard Medical School was not spared as the second wave of the medical malpractice crisis cycled through our nation in the early 1980s. Particularly noteworthy to the Harvard Risk Management Department was the costly impact of the Medical School's Anesthesia Department. That department's leadership was told, "You must do something to greatly improve your present rate of medical liability." To that department's credit, they did do something quick and dramatic. The Harvard Medical School Department of Anesthesia controlled nine separate departments at nine separate hospitals within their system. A committee was formed, and the past patient care incidents were studied to gain an understanding of where the greatest cause(s) of those incidents occurred. Their findings showed that basic patient monitoring practices were thought to be so important in accident prevention that they must become mandatory. The creation of mandatory basic monitoring guidelines in the practice of medicine had never been done before.

The Harvard Medical School Department of Anesthesia devised seven specific, detailed, mandatory standards for minimal patient monitoring during anesthesia at its nine component teaching hospitals. I see those minimal standards like seven lines drawn in the sand that said to every department anesthesiologist, "Doctor, if you cross one of those lines, we cannot help you." By going where no other medical organization had ever gone before, they became professional heretics.

Individually and collectively, none of those minimal standards appeared to be asking too much of a dedicated anesthesiologist. Harvard risk management got the quick and dramatic result they were seeking. Within one year, the medical liability rate for that anesthesia department showed a wonderful improvement. But improved quality patient care was not the perspective taken by organized medicine.

The Harvard Anesthesia Department event demonstrated rapid and dramatic patient safety improvement by using "a few fundamental, minimal standards that would be achievable in the smallest community hospital." That achievement occurred almost thirty years ago, but there is no evidence it was adopted nationwide. Why those live saving, minimal standards were not rapidly adopted in every hospital department of anesthesia is a question that this book intends to answer.

Note: I continue to consider this to be one of the most important articles in the entire medical literature regarding patient safety during the past four decades, and I discovered this gem during my research efforts for writing First, Do No Harm (my first book) in 2003. I reviewed every issue of the Journal of American Medical Association (JAMA) between 1949 and 2003.

Second Event:
Incidence of Adverse Events and Negligence in Hospitalized Patients – Results of the Harvard Medical Practice Study I, Brennan, T.A., M.P.H., M.D., Leape, Lucian, M.D., et al, New England Journal of Medicine, Feb. 1991 (Part 1 of three articles).

Brennan and Leape were co-leaders of a team of Harvard School of Public Health researchers who began their study in 1986 of thousands of patient medical records in upstate New York hospitals for four years that culminated in the originally accepted estimate of 98,000 needless hospital deaths annually in 1990. Several smaller studies had also been conducted, but this study was by far the largest, and most widely acclaimed and accepted.

Institute of Medicine (IOM) would form two committees that would adopt the findings of this study and their efforts would culminate in To Err Is Human, 2000, (Dr. Leape would be a member of one of those committees). Special note should be taken that this team of Harvard School of Public Health researchers were delegated sufficient *authority* by the state of New York that allowed them complete access to individual hospital patient records, and that *authority* extended for a period of four years.

Third Event:
Congress: Healthcare Quality Improvement Act – 1986 (HCQIA-86)

A Republican Congress, in their efforts to support Organized Medicine, a major source of financial support, created two distinctly different quality of patient care *improvements* that if ever examined in detail each would demonstrate increased protection for doctors who provide negligent care to far too many patients.

- **Medical peer review** was made secret, and all 50 state legislatures, like dominos, rapidly adopted this secure veil of secrecy, thereby allowing every hospital medical staff to

proclaim the effective use of medical peer review while never having to prove evidence of such.
- **National Practitioner Data Bank (NPDB)** was created in 1986, but only became *functional* in 1990. But "functional" is an inexact word to use when discussing the functionality of the NPDB. The secrecy allowed for the NPDB even exceeds that of medical peer review, and therefore the effectiveness of the NPDB has been nonexistent in the real world of negligent patient care. Details of such ineffectiveness will be provided in **2014.**

President Reagan and the Republican Congress of 1986 had, and continue to have, no idea of how harmful those two well-intended congressional determinations have been fundamentally counterproductive to improving the quality of patient care and patient safety. American Medical Association (AMA) and other medical and surgical specialties obtained the levels of secrecy regarding practitioner misconduct in instances of questionable patient care they had long fought for.

These two widely diverse events that took place in the same year will hopefully prepare those interested in their Healthcare Delivery System for what has taken place in all the efforts to try to make medical care safer during the next four decades. Congress with its combined Senate and House committees, and subcommittees on health, states with their multiple health agencies, Organized Medicine with its wide array of societies and associations, and the enormous Quality of Healthcare and Patient Safety Army of experts have succeeded in establishing a patient safety track record of abject failure.

Demonstration of how ineffective all efforts to improve the quality of healthcare, and patient safety can be found in a combination of To Err Is Human failures, and the past quarter century of needless hospital deaths track record. To Err Is Human failures include the promise to "reduce the annual estimates of needless hospital deaths by 50% in five years" from that original annual estimate of only 98,000, and the recognition that the current Healthcare Delivery System was in fact a *non-system*, but the failure to recognize the importance of that critical recognition.

But the worst was yet to come; every new estimate of needless hospital deaths annually has been greater than all previous estimates for the past 25 years, thus an established track record of failure, and no identifiable rationale for why. But timelines are intended to be sequential, and a few examples of the early beginnings of the Quality of Healthcare and Patient Safety Army of experts, and related contributory events are necessary in order to begin to understand "Where are we now, and how did we get here?" Anyone who seeks to substantially change an enormous, complex *system* they cannot first describe in detail disregard logic while resulting in a confirmation of Einstein's definition of insanity.

Due to the size and scope of the many various sources involved in efforts to improve the quality of healthcare and patient safety during the past several decades the timeline format used thus far will be altered. Each major source (Federal, states, Organized Medicine, and some of the many separate components of the Quality of Healthcare and Patient Safety Army of experts) will be presented separately in the hope for more clarity.

The premise of the remaining chapters of this book is to attempt to illustrate the enormous amount of time, money, and effort expended by thousands of highly educated individuals seeking to improve the quality of healthcare and patient safety, and the overwhelming evidence of so little success.

The documented efforts of each specific entity of each of those four major sources will demonstrate the same consistent failures of recognition, and/or the ability to explain;

- Each state's responsibility to create and maintain an effective Healthcare Delivery System due to the combined facts that all medical care is local and states license doctors to practice medicine.

- Absence of an organization structure necessary for the existence of clear points of authority, and sufficient delegated authority required for meaningful accountability.
- Why the absence of an organizational structure makes it impossible to disseminate effective patient safety measures effectively throughout all of the hospitals, and surgery centers, in the nation, in spite of countless promises to do exactly that.
- Inability to explain why every new estimate of needless hospital deaths has been greater than all previous estimates for the past 25 years.
- Why each state lacks the ability to provide accurate and specific numbers on needless hospital deaths in their hospitals or surgery centers, and identify the source and methods used of authority that responds to such tragic events.

The timeline's altered format continues with the addition of the fourth major source of efforts to improve the quality of healthcare and patient safety.

Congress & Federal Government

Congress
  Senate: 3 Committees and multiple Sub-Committees dealing with Health
  House: 7 Committees and multiple Sub-Committees dealing with Health.

Federally created Healthcare Agencies
Department of Health and Human Services (1979) 12 Divisions
  (Entities selected that are germane to this publication)
  Centers for Medicare & Medicaid Services (CMS) formerly Health Care Financing Administration (HCFA)
  Office of Inspector General (OIG)

Office of Evaluation and Inspections (OEI) 6 Offices
Quality of Healthcare and Patient Safety Agencies created by Congress
Agency for Health Research and Quality (AHRQ) originally named Agency for Healthcare Policy & Research became a division of DHHS (1989)
Institute of Medicine (IOM) now **National Academy of Medicine** (1970)
National Practitioner Data Bank (NPDB) (1986)
National Quality Forum (1999)
Patient-Centered Outcomes Research Institute (PCORI) (2010)

Malcolm Baldrige National Quality Improvement Award
Institute of Medicine

1970 Institute of Medicine (IOM) became a component of the **National Academy of Science**. [Note: IOM became **National Academy of Medicine, April 2015,** but will be referred to as IOM throughout this book]

1997 Institute of Medicine: Began studies resulting in first a report *To Err Is Human* (1999) and in 2000 the first in a series of six books between 2000 and 2004.

1999 Institute of Medicine: To Err Is Human report was first released. That report was based upon the Brennan, Leape, et.al., 1990 estimate of 98,000 needless hospital deaths annually, and promised to reduce that estimate by 50% in five years. That report was also the first public recognition that the Healthcare Delivery System was in fact a non-system.

2000 Institute of Medicine: To Err Is Human was released in book form and contained 9 recommendations, and the following prediction, "Given current knowledge about the magnitude of the problem, the committee believe it would be irresponsible to expect anything less than a 50 percent reduction in errors over five years." [Note: 2013 estimate of needless hospital deaths was quadruple the estimate of 98,000 needless hospital deaths used in the To Err Is Human report]

2001 Institute of Medicine: Crossing the Quality Chasm was the second book published, joining To Err Is Human, and four additional books published between 2000 and 2004 and referred to as the Crossing the Quality Chasm series. That series of books contains 53 recommendations.

2003 Rand Corporation "Only a fundamental redesign of the health system will improve the situation." Elizabeth McGlynn, PhD (second recognition that the current healthcare *system* is, and has always been, a non-system, devoid of any systematic characteristics) The Quality of Health Care Delivered to Adults in the United States, NEJM, Vol. 348, No. 26, June 26, 2003, pp. 2635-2645.

Agency for Healthcare Research and Quality (AHRQ) (formerly Agency for Healthcare Policy and Research)

1989 Agency for Healthcare Research and Quality (AHRQ) mission is to produce evidence to make health care safer, higher quality, more accessible, equitable, and affordable, and to work within the U.S. Department of Health and Human Services and with other partners to make sure that the evidence is understood and used.

2008 AHRQ Director Dr. Carolyn Clancy, in her Performance Budget Submission for Congressional Justification for fiscal year 2008 stated, "We are seeing results of efforts to improve quality of care. AHRQ released the fourth annual reports focusing on quality of and disparities in healthcare in America. Overall, the review of forty core quality measures found a 3.1 percent increase in the quality of care – the same rate of improvement as the previous two years."

2012 AHRQ WebM&M, morbidity and mortality rounds on web. Dr. Robert Wachter's conversation with Richard Boothman, JD, March 2012

Mr. Boothman is the chief risk officer for the University of Michigan Health System.

Mr. Boothman. "A simple example is a comment that one of our surgeons made to me about two weeks ago. He said to me, "I was on faculty here six months, at only six months I could give you a short list of people I never wanted to be in the operating room with." That information is well known. Who are those people that everybody knows about who may be unsafe or may be challenged? Maybe we need to get our arms around them and make them safer. In that conversation I slid a legal pad across the table and I said, "write them down and I'll start looking at them," and he wouldn't write them down. That's a complex question about what to do next."

2015 AHRQ Staff: 314 Budget $0.43 billion (over $2 billion in five years)

1999 National Quality Forum (NQF) was established pursuant to the recommendations of the President's Advisory Commission on Consumer Protection and Quality. Under the National Technology Transfer and Advancement Act, NQF is recognized as a private sector standard-setting organization charged to review performance measures, best practices, and serious reportable events, and to endorse those as national standards.

2008 "Patient safety measures in our nation are improving only 1 % each year." Janet Corrigan, President/CEO. That same year Dr. Corrigan participated in a joint presentation with Dr. Leape at the **National Patient Safety Foundation** annual meeting, but to a select, non-public audience. They spoke on, "Reflection on the Past 10 Years: Why Have We Not Gotten Further?"

2010 Patient-Centered Outcomes Research Institute (PCORI) was created by Congress. The Patient Centered Outcomes Research Institute is authorized by Congress to conduct research to provide information about the best available evidence to help patients and their healthcare providers make more informed decisions. PCORI's research is intended to give patients a better understanding of the prevention, treatment and care options available, and the science that supports those options.

Mission: The Patient-Centered Outcomes Research Institute helps people make informed healthcare decisions, and important healthcare delivery and outcomes, by producing and promoting high integrity, evidence-based information that comes from research guided by patients, caregivers and the broader healthcare community.

Quasi-Congressional/Federal Healthcare Agencies
(Contracted Services with little or no Oversight)

Joint Commission (JC)

Joint Commission was "hatched" by the **AMA, ACS, ACP,** and **AHA** in 1951, but the **JC,** as we have known it for the past fifty years, was "created" by **Congress** along with **Medicare,** and **Medicaid in 1965.**

1965 **JC,** as stated in earlier comments regarding the passage of **Medicare** and **Medicaid,** was *deemed* (a contractual basis with little oversight) to certify hospitals qualified to receive **Medicare** payments for patient services. That certifying responsibility required the **JC** to *inspect* each hospital seeking such payments on a regularly prescribed schedule. The question today is, how well has that process been fulfilled?

But the Joint Commission has a highly checkered past as demonstrated by the following two articles, and described in more details in my previous three books.

Joint Commission 1988 Wall Street Journal

Walt Bogdanich, writing in a front-page article, gave a description of the Joint Commission that was a far cry from Organized Medicine's description of their benevolent standard-bearer and dispenser of the hospital world's highest "seal of approval." He claimed that the Joint Commission's standard operating procedure at that time was to accept virtually every hospital that applied for accreditation. In addition, the Joint Commission rarely, if ever, disciplined or punished hospitals that violated its standards. Perhaps, suggested Bogdanich, that was because the commission's multi-million dollar budget was primarily covered by hospital fees for accreditation.

At that time, hospitals were given at least a one-month advance notice of an on-site inspection, and the results of that inspection were kept confidential. Furthermore, for a hefty sum, the commission sold consultant packages advising hospitals how to pass an inspection.

A survey of the Joint Commission data for the period 1986 to 1988 showed that of 5,208 accredited hospitals, 51% did not have adequate procedures for reviewing surgery; 56% did not properly monitor or evaluate how well the medical staff in different departments gave care; and more than 40% were cited for violations of safety standards while keeping their accreditation. As Bogdanich pointed out, one New York hospital was closed by the state for violations immediately after it had been accredited by the Joint Commission. Shortly thereafter, New York State decided to stop using the Joint Commission to accredit its hospitals.

Following the adverse publicity, the Joint Commission promised to reform. New committees were formed. New people took office. New standards for patient safety and medical/healthcare error reduction in hospitals were written. It was promised that a random, unannounced inspection policy would be implemented. A 20 member standards review task force was formed to pinpoint where accreditation standards were most relevant to the safety and quality of patient care and to recommend the elimination or modification of standards that did not contribute to good patient care. Press releases trumpeted new standards for office-based surgeries, for patient restraint, for treatment of specific diseases, and a dozen other projects.

2002 Chicago Tribune

Reporters Michael Berens and Bruce Japsen did another in-depth investigation of the organization. They found even more shocking flaws in the system, which now involves fewer hospitals 4,800, but more care facilities 14,000. The cost of being accredited has risen to $40,000 and the pre-investigation consultation cost $10,000. Instead of giving hospitals a month of lead time before inspections, the commission now gives them three months. Joint Commission allows hospitals to choose the patient files to be reviewed; obviously, these will all be success stories with happy endings.

The fact is that the Joint Commission is accountable to no one – not to government or to patients – and this lack of accountability has allowed it to grow out of control. After more than 50 years of being the profession's answer to self-regulation and 40 years of being the federal government's seal of approval for Medicare, the Joint Commission has developed cracks in its wall of secrecy that are finally allowing the public a glance at what regulation and standardization of the profession by the profession amounts to.

For instance, the Joint Commission has created a list of "sentinel events" that are supposed to act like smoke detectors. Any one event will bring the Joint Commission investigators to a hospital. They define a sentinel event is "an unexpected occurrence involving death or serious physical or psychological injury."

A recent sentinel event occurred at Children's Hospital in St. Louis when 90 cases of salmonella poisoning were reported. The kitchen was shut down for 10 days while an investigation was conducted. Once the kitchen was cleaned and a couple of food handlers were dismissed, the investigation ended. Will the incident show up in the Joint Commission's records? Incredibly, since 1995, the Joint Commission has documented only 12 cases of preventable hospital-borne infections from the thousands of healthcare facilities it monitors.

In 2002, infections in a Florida hospital caused 18 deaths and brought out more than 100 litigants against the medical center. All of the litigants had undergone cardiac surgery and had become disabled as a result of infection. The Joint Commission's sent investigators, but their findings were withheld from those who were infected. "If we want any modicum of cooperation from the hospitals, they have to feel we're not going to put investigative findings right out on the street," said the Joint Commission president, Dr. Dennis O' Leary. One of the litigants responded, "It's outrageous. This infection has destroyed my life, but I'm being treated like I'm the bad guy."

Summary

Congress has created multiple agencies dedicated to improving the quality of healthcare and patient safety, and provided *deeming responsibility* to other non-federal agencies to certify hospitals to receive Medicare payments. And the collective results of all of the above are:

- Every new estimate of needless hospital deaths has been greater than all previous estimates for the past 25 years.
- No recognition by any of the identified agencies, or others, regarding each state's responsibility to create and maintain an effective Healthcare Delivery System.
- The current *system* has long been recognized to be a *non-system*, (devoid of any *systematic characteristic*) thereby obstructing efforts to introduce patient safety measures throughout the current Healthcare Delivery System.

Quality of Care and Patient Safety army of experts is enormous, and their leaders have been nationally and internationally known for decades through their books, articles, and for some, their organizations, and annual conferences. Yet few people who are not actively engaged in their efforts would recognize their names or Federal Agencies and organizations. I am a member of the fairly new **Society to Improve Diagnosis in Medicine (SIDM),** but the leadership of that organization won't speak to me at meetings because I have challenged publicly challenged them regarding their refusal to recognize each state's responsibility.

Quality of Care Army Report Card

Federal Quality & Patient Safety Agencies

	Created	Years
National Academy of Medicine (NAM) (formerly Institute of Medicine (IOM)	1970	48
Agency for Healthcare Research & Quality (AHRQ)	1987	31
National Practitioner Data Bank (NPDB)	(1986) 1990	28
National Quality Forum (NQF)	1999	19
Patient Centered Outcomes Research Insti. (PCORI)	2010	_8_
Total Years		134
Billions of Tax Payer's money		

Current Estimates

Medical Errors – 3rd Leading Cause of Deaths – Heart Disease – Cancer
Every New Estimate of Needless Hospital Deaths has been Greater than All Previous Estimates for Past 28 Years

What's Been Missing?

Current Healthcare Delivery System was recognized in To Err Is Human to actually be a Non-System (devoid of any Systematic Characteristics) in 2000, but that recognition has been ignored.

States responsibility to create and maintain an effective healthcare delivery system has been unrecognized by everyone at every level of efforts to improve the quality of healthcare and patient safety.

I repeat, the subject is not America's Healthcare Delivery System, or South Carolina's Healthcare Delivery System. The subject is Your and Your Loved One's Healthcare Delivery System, and no state governor or legislator, past or present, has every recognized their responsibility to create, and maintain, an effective system for their citizens. I am looking for people who want to begin to not ask, but demand that meaningful change begin where it can do the most good, in state capitols.

CHAPTER 10

What Other Experts Are Saying

So far, each reader has been asked to rely on my contrarian views regarding their and their loved ones' Healthcare Delivery System therefore I thought it would be helpful to include the published views of other sources from within the current "system".

2009 Drs. Berwick, Gawande, Fisher, and McClellan, *New York Times* **OP-ED,**

"But all medicine is local. And until a community confronts what goes on in its own population – to the point of actually seeking the data and engaging those who can solve the problem – nothing will change."

Find The Black Box, Chapter 1, page 1 offered my response to their comment regarding the need for community activity.

"From the horses' mouths!" I assume no one will wish to dispute those words from such impeccable medical sources. But I see two problems with any community trying to find the ability necessary to confront such matters. First, these four experts fail to explain exactly how any community can *confront, obtain data,* and *engage those who can solve the problem*? Second, since more people are needlessly dying in our nation's hospitals now than were dying needlessly over twenty years ago, where might community members engage those who can SOLVE THE PROBLEM? More importantly, can those four medical experts identify such a health care "problem solver" in any community in the nation? I submit that there are too many 'Quality of Health

Care Experts' out there who are speaking out of both sides of their mouths - but that is just my opinion.

2013 Dr. Berwick's Institute for Healthcare Improvement 25th Annual National Forum, Orlando, FL

I was the guest of Dr. Gary Kaplan, CEO Virginia Mason Health System, and IHI Board Chairman, and I was allowed to attend the CEO and Leadership Summit all-day program based upon the High-Impact Leadership 35 page White Paper which invited feedback.

My Response Critique, provided here, was delivered to Maureen Bisognano, IHI CEO and President, and Dr. Stephen Swensen, Professor, Mayo Clinic, and Medical Director, Leadership and Organization Development, Mayo Clinic.

"We invite feedback on what is helpful, what is missing, and what are the next steps for building strong leadership and more reliable improvement in patient experience, cost of care, and population health."

I accept your invitation to provide you with my perspective of what is missing in your White Paper – and – what has always been missing in our nation's entire healthcare delivery system.

What's missing: Organizational structure with clearly defined points of authority, and delegated authority, all necessary for accountability to take place as rapidly as possible, and as near to the patient care event as possible.

High -Impact Leadership White Paper contains approximately 150 uses of the words Leaders, Leadership, and some form of Organization. I challenge each participant in the creation of this White Paper to describe, in detail, the organizational structure of their state's healthcare delivery system, name each component, describe how each component functions, and how at least some of these components function in some form of organizational unity, i.e., as a "system".

My military career as a Wing Headquarters Squadron Commander (1956 -57), and my surgical career as a hospital department chairman and member of the medical staff executive committee demonstrated the stark contrast between having a Leadership position with sufficient delegated authority necessary for accountability to take place as the need arose (military), and the complete absence of those vital elements (healthcare delivery system).

A simple test should suffice to illustrate what is, and always has been missing in our current healthcare delivery system. Identify any hospitals where the medical staff chiefs of services have been delegated sufficient authority necessary for patient care accountability to take place rapidly, and as near as possible to the questionable patient care event.

Leaders lacking sufficient delegated authority are Leaders in name only, and are incapable of providing true Leadership. Organizations without clearly defined points of authority and delegated authority are likewise organizations in name only.

The CEO and Leadership Summit provided the ingredients necessary for a true test to judge the ability to introduce the many positive patient safety measures throughout a specific healthcare delivery system. How long would it take to introduce all of the quality of healthcare and patient safety measures currently found at the Cleveland Clinic and various Cincinnati hospitals into every hospital and surgery center in Ohio?

In the past quarter of a century the annual estimate of needless hospital deaths has quadrupled, with an additional 10-20 times number of patients medically harmed, though not fatally. That sad statistic should be the standard every quality of healthcare organization is judged by.

IHI Pres/CEO Bisognano declined my offer of a copy of my book *Find The Black Box*, but Dr. Swensen accepted my offer, and later sent me the following message; Ira, wonderful book...your work is impressive. Thanks, Steve.

2009 Dr. Leape, along with **Janet Corrigan, NQF CEO** and a co-editor of **IOM To Err Is Human** gave a presentation at the **National Patient Safety Foundation** annual meeting in Washington

DC entitled *"Reflections on the Past 10 Years: Why Have We Not Gotten Further?"* Unfortunately, their joint presentation was only offered to an exclusively select group. Also unfortunate, their "reasons" for the monumental failure to even come close to their promised five-year goal in improving the quality of healthcare by reducing the annual rate of needless hospital deaths by 50% was NEVER MADE PUBLIC.

2013 A New, Evidence-based Estimate of Patient Harms Associated with Hospital Care, John T. James, PhD, Journal of Patient Safety, September.

Article Abstract: Using a weighted average of the 4 studies, a lower limit of 210,000 deaths per year was associated with preventable harm in hospitals. Given limitations in the search capability of the Global Trigger Tool and the incompleteness of medical records on which the Tool depends, the true number of premature deaths associated with preventable harm to patients was estimated at more than 400,000 per year. Serious harm seems to be 10- to 20-fold more common than lethal harm.

Conclusions: The epidemic of patient harm in hospitals must be taken more seriously if it is to be curtailed. Fully engaging patients and their advocates during hospital care, systematically seeking the patients' voice in identifying harms, transparent accountability for harm, and intentional correction of root causes of harm will be necessary to accomplish this goal.

2013 How Many Die From Medical Mistakes in U.S. Hospitals? Marshall Allen, ProPublica, September.

Excerpts: Dr. Lucian Leape, a Harvard pediatrician who is referred to as the "father of patient safety" was on the committee that wrote the "To Err Is Human" report. He told ProPublica that he has confidence in the four studies and the estimate by James.

Members of the Institute of Medicine committee knew at the time that their estimate of medical errors was low, he said. "It was based on a rather crude method compared to what we do now," Leape said. Plus, medicine has become much more complex in recent decades, which leads to more mistakes, he said.

Dr. David Classen, one of the leading developers of the Global Trigger Tool, said the James study is a sound use of the tool and a "great contribution." He said it's important to update the numbers from the "To Err Is Human" report because in addition to the obvious suffering, preventable harm leads to enormous financial costs.

Dr. Marty Makary, a surgeon at The Johns Hopkins Hospital whose book "Unaccountable" calls for greater transparency in health care, said the James estimate shows that eliminating medical errors must become a national priority. He said it's also important to increase the awareness of the potential of unintended consequences when doctors perform procedure and tests. The risk of harm needs to be factored into conversations with patients, he said.

Leape, Classen and Makary all said it's time to stop citing the 98,000 number.

2012 Dr. Marty Makary *Unaccountable, What Hospitals Won't Tell You and How Transparency Can Revolutionize Health Care*

A hospital is no longer the community pillar I knew growing up, with its altruistic mission guiding its decisions. Hospitals have merged and transformed into giant corporations with little accountability – and they like it that way.

In 2010, a Harvard study published in the prestigious New England Journal of Medicine reported a finding well-known to medical professionals: as many as 25% of all patients are harmed by medical mistakes. What's even less known to the public is that over the past ten years, error rates have not come down, despite numerous efforts to make medical care safer.

Dr. Lucian Leape, at a national surgeon's conference opened the gathering's keynote speech by looking out over the audience of thousands and asking the doctors to "raise your hand if you know of a physician you work with who should not be practicing because he or she is dangerous." Every hand went up. Incredulous at this response, I took to asking the same question when ever I spoke at conferences. And I always got the same response. Every doctor knows about this problem – but few talk about it. Every day, people are injured or killed by medical mistake that might have been prevented with a modicum of adherence to standardize guidelines. The silence about the problem has paralyzed efforts to address it – until now. Medicine is its own culture. It has its own language, ethos, and code of justice. Doctors swear to do no harm. But on the job they soon absorb another unspoken rule: to overlook malpractice in their colleagues.

We all know the health care system is broken, burdening our families, businesses, and national debt. It needs common-sense reform.

The patients whose numbers came up with Dr. Hodad were just the unlucky victims of a system lacking in standardization, oversight, or ways to measure quality.

But watching Hodad in action made me realize that patient satisfaction was only half the story. Patients couldn't know what we staff in the operating room could see: that the man was dangerous, had poor judgment, and practice outdated medicine. Doctors work in a disjointed system with perverse incentives, little oversight, and a lot of haggling that goes on behind closed doors far from public view – kind of like Congress.

There were other, more powerful ways I was "educated" on the code of silence. Once in a hospital peer-review conference, I witnessed the futility of a brave doctors speaking up to condemn another doctor's careless decision to operate when the operation didn't meet criteria. The doctor at fault gave a justification that a courtroom would believe, but we all knew it was not true. It was a rare spectacle, yet nothing came out of it, except that the brave doctor who spoke up became a marked man. Throughout my training I witnessed several doctors run out of town because their honesty and outspokenness begin to poke the bear. In many ways, direct and indirect, I was taught that the code of silence was part of being a doctor.

Unlike aviation, hundreds of thousands of lives are lost each year due to preventable mistakes by doctors.

If we had more of it, the accountability visited on hospitals would revolutionize the quality of medical care in every city in America, dramatically reshaping our health care landscape.

Seeking accurate ways to measure patient outcomes has long been the holy grail of health care reform, the starting point for fixing our broken health care system.

As I listen to Dr. Leape talk about secret addictions and other common impairments, I realized that he wasn't just talking about doctors who simply have poor skills or bad judgment. This was an entirely different problem. He was talking about doctors affected by dependence problems and other physical and mental impairments.

That's when the problem of impaired physicians struck me as nothing less than a public health crisis. I did some more math. If, say, only 2% of the nation's one million doctors are seriously impaired by drugs, alcohol abuse, or other major impairments (and most experts agree that 2% is a low estimate), that means twenty thousand impaired doctors are practicing medicine. I asked, "What can be done about these few bad apples affecting so many people?" Dr. Leape smiled, and said, "The state medical boards take care of that."

Yet there are also grossly impaired physicians, doctors with horrible skills, hazardous judgment, ulterior your motive motives, or who suffer from substance-abuse or other problems that make them dangerous. Society ought to be able to deal with this better, not sweep it all under the rug. Doctoring is a stressful profession with easy access to drugs, so it's no mystery why doctors have substance abuse problems. In fact, rates of serious substance abuse and psychiatric disease among doctors are actually higher than that of other professions with similar educational background in socio-economic status.

However, based on Halsted's life and what I've seen in my career, I agree with others that 2% is a drastic understatement of the true incidence of impaired physicians.

One time, right after this notoriously bad surgeons run of six deaths, my friend was administrating in anesthesia for him. In front of all the operating room nurses and technicians, the patient asked my friend before going off to sleep, "Is my surgeon a good surgeon?" The operating room staff froze as their eyes popped out of their heads. They stared at my friend to see how he would deal with the direct question. "He's one of the four best heart surgeons we have here", he said with a smile. Luckily for my friend, the patient didn't follow up with, "And how many heart surgeons do you have here?"

Having inside knowledge about a risky doctor while trying to comfort his patient in preparation for surgery is a dilemma every health care provider knows all too well. I asked my friend if he ever thought about reporting this surgeon to someone. He laughed and asked, "Like who?"

The hospital administration loved this young heart surgeon, who was making a financial killing (pardon the pun) off his work. The senior partners were very protective of him as the youngest member of their group – after all, he took most of their weekend calls for them. He covered their holiday shifts and happily tended to whatever the senior surgeons did not like to do, such as operating on their obese patients for them. They cut the young doc tremendous slack whenever his complications were discussed at a peer-review conference, saying a patient's death was attributable to some extenuating patient circumstances. (That's right, they'd blame the victim.)

Such internal peer reviews are a little like the Russian parliament under Stalin. No matter how much discussion there is, the result seems foreordained. At these internal peer review conferences, complicated cases are reduced to biased two-to-three-minute summaries, and doctors who might raise probing questions are well aware that they can pay a heavy price for challenging their peers.

Doctors and nurses know of docs who are reckless, but it takes moving a mountain to do something about it. Not reporting incompetence among peers is part of medical culture and has been for centuries. Medicine is poorly policed.

How about the national doctors associations? Can they police their own time? As a member of several, only once have I ever heard of a program that tried to address impaired physicians, and that effort never picked up steam. After asking around, it became clear that the only time that a doctor's association would ever consider taking action against the doctor was if a state medical board had already done so. Hungry to grow their membership and collect annual dues, doctors' associations are historically passive when it comes to policing doctors (the AMA is actively recruiting to increase its membership, which is now declined to 15% of US doctors; membership cost $420 a year). Policing doctors is a job so messy no one wants to do it.

So, who is in charge of policing medical care in America? Every organization, institution, medical Association, and hospital administrator that have I have asked has told me that policing physicians is the real responsibility of state medical boards. So let's examine the role of state medical boards in American medicine.

State medical boards

Consider California. The Medical Board of California, like all others is responsible for licensing and disciplining physicians. On three different audits conducted during the 1980s, the California auto to general found that the board wasn't doing its job. Apart from that announcement, no further action was taken. The board went 18 years without another audit until 2003, when University of San Diego Law School Professor Julie D'Angelo Fellmeth became the medical board enforcement monitor. Then she blew a whistle. Testifying to a Senate committee in 2008 after years of trying to sound alarms, she said the Medical Board of California "routinely failed to promptly remove from work physician participants who tested positive for prohibited substances." The board had five out of five failed audit audits. Julie D'Angelo Fellmeth was let go. The Medical Board of California then went on doing whatever it does about impaired physicians, which is to say, not much.

Impaired physicians are a small minority of doctors who are very destructive and difficult to police. Knowingly or unknowingly, they cause a lot of harm. State medical boards are sometimes aware of them, but look the other way. Standards for doctors are local and vary widely state by state.

Nearly every doctor can name a doctor who needs to retire but won't – impaired doctors in their 90s who refused to leave the office even when they are no longer being paid. Why do we have this problem? The reason is there are no rules.

I can legally do anything. In fact, some varicose-vein removal centers in the United States are run by former OB/GYN doctors and others by psychiatrists; they were doctors looking to do something different and took a weekend course to learn how to do it. Putting aside how I get paid, I can do whatever I want in medicine with little to no accountability.

Being in the medical-errors field has decreased my threshold for shock. A New England Journal of Medicine study concluded that as many as 25% of all hospitalized patients will experience a preventable medical error of some kind. Almost everyone I talk to has a story about a friend or family member who was hurt, disfigured, are killed by medical mistake. Even me.

My research partner, Peter Pronovost, lost his father due to a medical error when Peter was in medical school. My medical partner, Dr. Patrick O'Kolo, lost his younger sister due to a medical error. My best friend's mom had her breast removed unnecessarily because she was mistakenly told she had stage-three breast cancer. After her procedure, her doctors told her the original report had a mistake – she had only had stage one and hadn't needed a breast removal after all. My grandfather died at age 60 from a condition called urosepsis, a preventable infection following a surgery he didn't even need. My brother has a wide scar on his back from his stitches popping open after a skin mole was removed; he thinks it was unavoidable bad luck, but I can tell the surgeon used stitches too weak to hold the skin together. My cousin worked with a cardiac surgeon and witness countless deaths from an impaired physician. I myself was misdiagnosed with a knee problem in medical school.

Listening to Peter and many friends who have similar stories, I realize that the patent these patients suffered not just from their botched treatments but from the knowledge that their misfortune need never have happen. For them, talking about medical mistakes is part of their healing. But our system wants to sweep them under the rug and keep them quiet. I sometimes hear egregious stories from people who preface their accounts with, "Please keep this just between you and may, because I signed a waiver saying that I would never talk about this." When a doctor or hospital does harm a patient, this settlement offer from the hospital often contains a confidentiality clause (a.k.a. "a gag rule"). In fact, in any case of gross neglect, hospital lawyers will aggressively pursue victims or their surviving family to settle out-of-court quickly in order to stem off a malpractice suit – provided they agree never to speak about what happened, even if one has been disfigured, maimed, or killed.

In order to get a handle on the widespread epidemic of medical mistakes, we need more conversation about them, not less.

There are bad doctors and impaired doctors, but the problem of doctors making repeated avoidable mistakes is a management problem.

Every health services researcher knows errors are common. Medical mistakes are not only far more common then they should be – they are a devastating cost burden on our health care system.

Patients under his care suffered because of these communication breakdowns. All this renegade needed was someone higher up the food chain – somebody with authority over his career – to take him aside and tell him to correct his attitude toward his coworkers. That never happened. He continued to terrorize his staff to the detriment of his patients.

How can we ensure accountability across the field of health care? In principle, most doctors and most hospital administrators agree that accountability is a good thing. But when I comes to being accountable themselves, they are often less enthusiastic. This is only human nature. Taking the extra effort to follow procedures meticulously or keep records of our performance can seem burdensome. And reducing your own accountability can protect your reputation and cover-up sins. You are freer to do what you want without having to bother about how other people will react. But a lack of accountability can alienate those who serve and fuel distrust. Moreover, knowing your accountable improves your performance.

Medicine is an institution as old as humanity. Its traditions are as hierarchical as those of the royals. And for centuries, doctors have enhanced their authority with mystery, keeping the workings of their profession opaque. But I am convinced that the new generation of doctors is poised to usher in a revolution of transparency, open-mindedness, and honesty. This generational shift may be just what is needed for medicine to end the secrecy that has historically permeated our profession. With younger doctors taking the lead, the culture is ripe for transformation if we can capitalize on this moment and push for reform from within.

My Response:
Accountability is a By-Product of AUTHORITY!

I couldn't stop showcasing so many of his quotes because they all mirror what I have been trying to present to any interested persons, decision-makers, and non-decision-makers, about what is missing, and has always been missing in our Health Care Delivery System.

The major difference between Dr. Makary's message and mine is that he sees the Problem, while I see both the Problem and the Solution. Hopefully, Dr. Makary is right, and the "culture" within the Medical Profession and the Hospital Administration Profession is changing, and becoming more receptive to considering fundamental change. Unfortunately, I am not as optimistic because I see no evidence of a desire, or even a recognition for a need to fundamentally change the direction of current efforts any where in the Quality of Health Care Experts' literature.

Sue or Forget It, and the response it receives from within the Quality of Health Care and Patient Safety Army, if and when coupled with Dr. Makary's well-received UNACCOUNTABLE and its quest for fundamental change, should indicate if the components of our current Health Care Delivery System are truly ready, willing, and able to confront these issues openly and in a meaningful manner.

Dr. Makary's book *UNACCOUNTABLE* was published in Nov. 2012, and a review appeared in the Wall Street Journal. When I read that review I went to Barnes & Noble, purchased a copy, and had it read in two days. When I closed his book I said I need to write another book, thus *Find The Black Box* was written, and published before Labor Day 2013.

Dr. Peter Pronovost

Dr. Pronovost is a practicing anesthesiologist and critical care physician, teacher, researcher, and international patient safety leader. He is a professor in the Johns Hopkins University School of Medicine (Departments of Anesthesiology and Critical Care Medicine, and Surgery) in the Bloomberg School of Public Health (Department of Health Policy and Management) and in the School of Nursing. He is also Medical Director for the Center for Innovation and Quality Patient Care, which supports quality and safety efforts at the Johns Hopkins Hospitals. In 2003.Dr. Pronovost established the Quality and Safety Research Group to advance the science of safety. Dr. Pronovost and his research team are dedicated to improving healthcare through methods that are scientifically rigorous, but feasible at the bedside. Dr. Pronovost holds a doctorate in clinical investigation from the Johns Hopkins Bloomberg School of Public Health.

Dr. Pronovost chairs the JCAHO ICU Advisory Panel for Quality Measures, the ICU Physician Staffing Committee for the Leapfrog Group, and serves on the Quality Measures Work Group of the National Quality Forum. He also serves in an advisory capacity to the World Health Organizations World Alliance for Patient Safety, and is leading WHO efforts to improve patient safety measurement, evaluation, and leadership capacity globally.

Time magazine, in 2008 named Dr. Pronovost one of the world's most influential people for his work in patient safety. The magazine's annual list recognizes people "whose power, talent or moral example is transforming our world." Dr. Pronovost also received the MacArthur Foundation Fellowship, commonly known as a "genius grant" in 2008.

The Pronovost Checklist:

Central venous catheters, or lines, are used for medications, blood, fluids or nutrition and can stay in for days or weeks. But bacteria can grow in the line in spread a type of infection to the bloodstream, which causes death in one out of five patients who contract it. This five-step checklist for doctors and nurses to use before inserting a line can prevent infections and death.

1. **Wash hands with soap and water or an alcohol cleanser.**
2. **Wear sterile clothing – a mask, gloves, and hair covering – and cover patient with a sterile drape, except for a very small hole where the line goes in.**
3. **Clean patient's skin with chlorhexidine (a type of soap) when the line is put in.**
4. **Avoid veins in arm and leg, which are more likely to get infected than veins in chest.**
5. **Check the line for infection each day and remove one no longer need it.**

The Secret to Fighting Infections: Dr. Peter Pronovost says it isn't that hard. If only hospitals would do it. (A WSJ conversation with Laura Landro)

Laura Landro WSJ: In your book you describe how hard it is to bring innovation and change to hospitals. What are the barriers to innervation?

Excerpts from Dr. Pronovost's responses

The main barriers are the lack of collaboration and a culture that is resistant to change. There is also a lack of systems integration.

In health care we need leadership to create a partnership between academic medicine and industry to pilot-test a new model.

The pilot who neglects a checklist before takeoff would not be allowed to fly, and most safe industries have transgressions that are firing offenses. But there hasn't been that kind of accountability in health care.

But physicians are often self-employed, have little training in teamwork and perhaps like all of us, are often overconfident about the quality of care they provide, believing things will go right rather than wrong.

Medicare provides a lot of money for training programs, and the federal government could require that we produce doctors in this country who are better trained in teamwork.

The Department of Health and Human Services has called for a 50% reduction in central line blood stream infections over three years, but in some states only 20% of hospitals have signed up.

What is perhaps most concerning is when I asked nurses, "If you saw a senior physician not comply with the checklist, would you speak up and would the physician comply?" Uniformly, the answer is no.

We have the knowledge about how to prevent infections, but it is just not being used are getting the attention it deserves, and that is just astounding.

Go back and read again Dr. Pronovost's "main barriers impeding positive change":

- A culture that is resistant.
- A lack of leadership to create partnerships.
- A lack of accountability.
- A lack of teamwork training.

What seems to be missing in his list of barriers to innovation?

Balancing "No Blame" with Accountability in Patient Safety
Robert M Wachter, M.D., and Peter J. Pronovost, M.D., Ph.D.
New England Journal of Medicine October1, 2009

Excerpts: Most errors are committed by good, hard-working people trying to do the right thing. Therefore, the traditional focus on identifying who is at fault is a distraction. It is far more productive to identify error-prone situations and settings and to implement systems that prevent caregivers from committing errors, catch errors before they cause harm, or mitigate harm from errors that do reach patients.

Most health care providers embrace the "no blame" model is a refreshing change from an errors landscape previously dominated by a malpractice system that was generally judged as punitive and arbitrary. And this shift has unquestionably born fruit. For example, rather than trying to perfect doctors' handwriting and memories, computerized systems catch medication errors before they reach patients.

Many health care organizations (including our own) have recognized that a unidimensional focus on creating a blame-free culture carries its own risks. But despite this recognition, finding the appropriate balance has been elusive, and few organizations have implemented meaningful systems of accountability, particularly for physicians.

Our failure to create real accountability for patient safety partly represents a fundamental misunderstanding regarding both how other, safer industries carry out their safety activities in the nature of errors.

On the other hand, physicians have traditionally been individual entrepreneurs, not employees, and thus are subject only to weak peer enforcement through medical staff structures. Not only do peers often recoil from disciplining "one of our own", but hospitals have been reluctant to punish physicians for fear of alienating them and losing the business they bring in.

As we enter the second decade of the safety movement, while the science regulating improving systems must continue to mature, the urgency of the task also demands that we stop averting our eyes from the need to balance no blame and accountability. "No blame" is not a moral imperative – and even if it seems that way to providers, it most definitely does not to patients and their advocates. Rather, it is a tactic to help us achieve ends (safe and high-quality care) for which we will, quite appropriately, be held accountable. Said another way, "no blame" is a tool, and often an extraordinarily useful one. But for some mature patient-safety practices, it is simply the wrong tool.

Finding this balance will be challenging. We recognize that reasonable people will differ on many of the details and that individual organizations may need customized approaches. To move the debate forward, we have chosen to be relatively explicit about suggested penalties for selected transgressions, hoping that organizations and caregivers will use them as "straw men" to generate their own policies. Our goal is simply to promote conversations and meaningful action. Until now, we have shuffled this issue to the bottom of the deck, preferring to work on easier, less contentious safety activities, such as computerization and checklists. It is time to raise this topic to the top of our agenda.

Part of the reason we must do this is that if we do not, other stakeholders, such as regulators and state legislatures, are likely to judge the reflective invocation of the "no blame" approach as an example of guild behavior – of the medical profession circling its wagons to avoid confronting harsh realities, rather than as a thoughtful strategy for attacking the root causes of most errors. With that as their conclusion, they will be predisposed to further intrude on the practice of medicine, using the blunt and often politicized sticks of the legal, regulatory, and payment systems,

Having our own profession unblinkingly deem some behaviors as unacceptable, with clear consequences, will serve as a vivid example of our professionalism and thus represent our best protection against such outside intrusions. But the main reason to find the right balance between "no blame" and individual accountability is that doing so will save lives. [Now for the subject of their quest for accountability.]

Prerequisites for Making the Choice to Punish Providers for Not Adhering to a Patient-Safety Practice, Using the Example of Hand Hygiene.

[**Note:** Now, reread their article while knowing that *hand hygiene* is the focal point of the authors' recognition of the need to better balance practitioner accountability with patient-safety practices. Hand hygiene is important and can save lives, just as Drs. Gawande and Pronovost checklists can save lives, but first must come far more meaningful authority and accountability within every hospital medical staff. 160 years after Semmelweis and hand hygiene remains a major patient safety hazard.]

Dr. Robert Wachter
Is the Patient Safety Movement in Danger of Flickering Out?
Dr. Robert Wachter Blog February 18, 2013

These should be the best of times for the patient safety movement. After all, it was concerns over medical mistakes that launched the transformation of our delivery and payment models, from one focused on volume to one that rewards performance. The new system (currently a work-in-progress) promises to put skin in the patient safety game has never before.

Yet I've never been more worried about the safety movement than I am today. My fear is that we will look back on the years between 2000 and 2012 as the Golden Era of Patient Safety, which would be okay if we'd fixed all the problems. But we have not.

A little history will illuminate my concerns. The modern patient safety movement began with the December 1999 publication of the IOM report on medical errors, which famously documented 44,000 – 98,000 deaths per year in the U.S. from medical mistakes, the equivalent of a large airplane crash each day. (To illustrate the contrast, we just passed the four-year mark since the last death in a U.S. commercial airline accident.) The IOM report sparked dozens of initiatives designed to improve safety: changes in accreditation standards, new educational requirements, public reporting, promotion of healthcare information technology, and more. It also spawned parallel movements focused on improving quality and patient experience.

As I walk around UCSF Medical Center today, I see an organization transformed by this new focus on improvement. In the patient safety arena, we deeply dissect 2-3 cases per month using a technique called Root Cause Analysis that I first heard about in

1999. The results of these analyses fuel "system changes" – also a foreign concept to clinicians until recently. We document and deliver care via a state-of-the-art computerized system. Our students and residents learn about QI and safety, and most complete a meaningful improvement project during their training. We no longer receive two years' notice of a Joint Commission accreditation visit; we receive 20 minutes notice. While the national evidence of improvement is mixed, our experience at UCSF reassures me: we've seen lower infection rates, fewer falls, fewer medication errors, fewer readmissions, better- train clinicians, and better systems. In short, we have an organization that is much better at getting better than it was a decade ago.

So, what's the problem? I see two major forces slackening the response to patient safety: clinician (particularly physician) burnout and strategic repositioning by delivery systems to deal with the Affordable Care Act. Like a harried parent rushing out to the car to drive the school carpool, only to discover that he's left his child in the house, we risk leaving behind our precious safety cargo if we fail to ensure that everybody is onboard as we rush headlong into the future.

Let's begin with burnout. When the patient safety field launched in 2000, one might have expected that physicians would be natural foes. After all, say "medical errors" to a practicing doctor and the Pavlovian response is likely to be "malpractice." This reflex made physicians unlikely patient safety enthusiasts, and it is axiomatic that nothing important happens in healthcare if physicians are not engaged.

Yet, by emphasizing systems problems – the "its not bad people, it's bad systems" argument – many physicians felt validated, some even intrigued and a few (like me) even inspired. Physicians turned from active resisters to, in many cases, real allies.

But the blizzard of new initiatives, – all well meaning but cumulatively overwhelming – thrust at busy clinicians has created overload. The problem, of course, is that nobody freed up the time to do all this new stuff. When commercial airline pilots recertify every year on a simulator, they do this on company time. When they spend

30 minutes completing a pre-flight checklist, their salary is assured. But for many physicians, these new task – learning a new way of thinking, implementing a checklist, or surviving the installation of a new IT system – are usually obligations on top of an already jam-packed day. Even for nurses, who generally are salaried, new mandates to scan bar codes or even to wash hands ate up precious minutes in days that already lacked much white space.

Although many clinicians have been gratified by their work in safety and quality, I'm afraid this additional work has contributed to high levels of burnout. A recent study in JAMA Internal Medicine documented burnout rates significantly higher than those of the rest of the U.S. population – with nearly half of physicians displaying symptoms of burnout. Obviously, patient safety initiatives are not the only cause of this burnout. But the effects on the safety field are very real.

While the statistics are troubling (and, as chair of the ABIM this year, I certainly hear from my share of unhappy doctors), the impact on patient safety really came home during my recent interview of Prof. Bryan Sexton, the Duke sociologists and the world's leading expert on patient safety culture. I had interviewed Bryan about culture six years ago for the federal website I edit, AHRQ WebM&M, and I thought it might be a good time to check back in. I approached the interview armed with a bunch of questions, covering things like Executive WalkRounds and teamwork training.

But within 10 minutes, I had scrapped all of my questions, because Bryan focused almost entirely on clinician burnout. In his work, he is seeing physicians and nurses so overwhelmed that getting them to think about anything else – safety, quality, teamwork – is nearly impossible. "It's like Maslow's hierarchy," he said, in that people aren't able to focus on higher needs until their basic needs are secured (the full interview will be published in the spring). Because of this, he has shifted his focus to improving "resiliency" – basically, helping docs and nurses restore joy in their work. As Dr. Richard Gunderman points out in a recent article in The Atlantic, while reducing dissatisfiers (hassles, bureaucracy, pay cuts, clunky IT systems) is important part of addressing a burnout, "the key (to combating physician burnout) is promoting professional wholeness, which flows from a full understanding of the real sources of fulfillment.

I cling to the hope that improving systems of care will bring fulfillment to clinicians (both from the work itself and the fruits of the labor), as it has for me and many of my colleagues. But it is important to recognize that for many clinicians (and not just the pre-retirement folks), this work is yet one more thing that stands between them and professional satisfaction.

The lack of evidence that all our hard work is paying off is also contributing to burnout. Several influential papers using the IHI's Global Trigger Tool methodology, have documented continued high rates of harm; one study of 10 hospitals in North Carolina showed no evidence of improvement between 2002 and 2007. On top of that, a steady drumbeat of studies (beautifully chronicled by Brad Flansbaum) demonstrates that nearly every policy intervention that we thought would work (readmission penalties, "no pay for errors", pay for performance, promotion of IT, resident duty-hour reductions) has either failed to work, are has led to negative unanticipated consequences. For people who have given their hearts and souls to making the system work better for patients, the result is more demoralization.

My second major concern about septic about patient safety stems from the Affordable Care Act (ACA), one of whose main goals, paradoxically, is to place a premium on value over volume. You'd think that the patient safety field would benefit from such a law (which also includes significant new spending on safety), and perhaps it will... eventually. But in the short term, the ACA is yet another speed bump on the road to a safe system

Just as physicians are overwhelmed and distracted, so too are hospital CEOs and boards. As the healthcare system lurches from its dysfunctional model to a (God willing) better place, healthcare leaders are scrambling to be sure that their organizations have seats when the music stops. The C-suite and boardroom conversations that, a few years ago, were focused on how to make systems better and safer now center on whether to become Accountable Care Organizations, how to achieve alignment with the medical staff, what the insurance exchange will mean for our reimbursement, and the like. To the degree that people remain interested in improving value, here too the emphasis has shifted from the numerator of the value equation (quality, safety, patient experience) to the denominator: cutting cost.

Dr. Gary Kaplan, CEO of Virginia Mason Health System in Seattle and probably the most admired hospital leader in the country, recently reflected on the state of patient safety in a note to the board of the Lucian Leape Institute at the National Patient Safety Foundation (we're both on the LLI board).

Gary wrote, "(The) reduction in reimbursement and increasing consolidation threatens to make the focus on economics, size, and market competitiveness take precedent over getting better in terms of quality and safety. This will be in part because the 'line of sight' from senior leaders to the front lines of care will be even more distant."

We simply must reorganize our healthcare systems to deliver the highest-value care. Of course, this will require big picture, strategic planning – new relationships, new institutions, new IT systems, and more. It will also depend on the creation of a bottom-up culture that allows those who deliver the care to improve it. Together, this is an awfully full agenda for both leaders and clinicians, and it is a noble one.

But as we proceed, we must remember that healthcare is delivered by real humans, working in organizations that are led by other real humans. Ignoring the pressures that both groups are under may lead us to create lovely systems and dazzling org charts for organizations that continue to harm and kill. In other words, we risk the dystopian world that the great healthcare futurist Ian Morrison has warned of, one in which our hospitals and clinics have the anatomy of high-performing organizations, but not the physiology.

Dr. Wachter asked himself, and others, a profound question, "**Is the Patient Safety Movement in Danger of Flickering Out?**" But did he answer his own question, and if so, how, and how well?

Reread his first two paragraphs. Will the years between 2000 and 2013 become the "Golden Era of Patient Safety" because "they" have fixed all the problems? I think not.

Dr. Wachter sees two major forces slackening the response to patient safety: clinician burnout and strategic repositioning by delivery systems to deal with the Affordable Care Act. I see much lacking in those two 'major forces' as the true causes for worry.

Later in his article Dr. Wachter quotes Dr. Gary Kaplan, CEO of Virginia Mason Health System in Seattle, "(The) reduction in reimbursement and increasing consolidation threatens to make the focus on economics, size, and market competitiveness take precedent over getting better in terms of quality and safety. This will be in part because the 'line of sight' from senior leaders to the front lines of care will be even more distant."

And then Dr. Wachter closes with, "But as we proceed, we must remember that healthcare is delivered by real humans, working in organizations that are led by other real humans. Ignoring the pressures that both groups are under may lead us to create lovely systems and dazzling org charts for organizations that continue to harm and kill. In other words, we risk the dystopian world that the great healthcare futurist Ian Morrison has warned of, one in which our hospitals and clinics have the anatomy of high-performing organizations, but not the physiology."

Dr. Wachter's soliloquy illustrates the Quality of Health Care Army of Expert's angst, while simultaneously demonstrating their complete failure to recognize every state's obligatory role to create and maintain the organizational structure he (Dr. Wachter) eludes to in his last paragraph. Quality of Health Care Army of Experts give full meaning to, "They can't see the forest for the trees!"

My answer to, **"Is the Patient Safety Movement in Danger of Flickering Out?"** is, not only is it 'flickering out', it has been 'flickering out' since its inception because of those experts' failure to recognize the states' responsibility. I believe there is a fairly simple test to support my conclusion; See if even one of our over forty schools of public health have a department head, or even a professor, who has written, taught, or even spoke on the states' responsibility regarding the Health Care Delivery System. "Experts" can't realize the potential importance of a key element they have never recognized. And nowhere in the Quality of Health Care Army of Experts literature will one find any evidence of their recognition of each state's responsibility. No school of public health will want to take that test.

I want to share a brief, but most informative, one-on-one conversation I had here in Greenville, South Carolina, with Dr. Wachter, who is professor of Medicine and Chief of the Division of Hospital Medicine at the University of California—San Francisco, and the person who coined the term "hospitalist" (more on this later). Dr. Wachter's presentation at Greenville Hospital System on September 30, 2010, was open to the public, and he was introduced as "one of the premier experts in the world regarding patient safety."

Dr. Wachter's presentation was entitled, "What We Need to Know and Do to Cure Our Epidemic of Medical Mistakes." I was the first person to capture his attention as he concluded his remarks and descended from the stage. We stood shoulder to shoulder close to the side of the steps to the stage and had the following cordial exchange (I also gave him a copy of Misdiagnosed!):

IW: "Dr. Wachter, you speak of systems errors, and in my two books I speak of individual practitioner errors. If we brought the two together we would really have something." Then I asked, "How do you get your system of systems errors to all of the hospitals in the nation?"

Dr. Wachter: "That's a problem."

IW: "I can solve that problem."

Dr. Wachter: [Silence]

Because others were waiting to speak with Dr. Wachter, I stepped aside and quietly left the room; but that brief exchange I just shared with "one of the premier experts in the world regarding patient safety" stayed with me.

I now want to share an email exchange between Dr. Wachter and I the Monday following our brief meeting.

On Oct 4, 2010, at 8:47 AM, Dr. Ira Williams wrote:

Dr Wachter,

    I thoroughly enjoyed your presentation and our brief conversation. I also read Balancing "No Blame" and I feel I now have a far more clear understanding of how our individual approaches to making HC safer both differ and benefit each other.
    Our HC system can never be what it should be until and unless we vastly improve Systems Errors and Practitioner Errors. I can provide a system of medial peer review fair to both doctor and patient that will enhance your efforts directed toward the other class of medical errors.
    I can also provide a system for getting those patient care improvements into all of our nation's hospitals.
    In Balancing "No Blame" you and Dr Pronovost say, "Our goal is simply to promote conversations and meaningful action. Is there room in your big Patient Safety tent for me?
    It is very easy for those who do not know me to judge me in a harsh and negative manner. I hope some day to be considered one of the best friends your profession has ever had. I hope you will consider my offerings in MISDIAGNOSED! from that perspective. I know how and where to make real HC patient safety happen. I would love to join you in conversation and meaningful action. We must reverse the twenty-year trend of needless hospital deaths.

Sincerely and respectfully,

October 4, 2010 12:54:50 PM EDT
    Thanks, Dr. Williams. I read your book on the way home. You make some important points and I agree that peer review is a critical, and mostly neglected, component of patient safety.
    I'll keep you in mind for appropriate opportunities, but don't have any right now.

Best regards.
—Bob

I have never heard from Dr. Wachter since even though he has been conducting interviews for AHRQ for many years he has never asked to interview me.

[**Note:** I have met face-to-face briefly with Drs. Berwick, Leape, Pronovost and Wachter, and I have had direct contact with Drs. Gawande, and Makary, and several of them have accepted copies of at least one of my books. Yet none of those doctors who make every copy of the most important Patient Safety Experts lists have commented on my recognition of each state's responsibility to create and maintain an effective Healthcare Delivery System. Drs. Berwick, Gawande, Fisher, and McClellan's joint recognition that *all medical care is local* in 2009 was a very positive step in the right direction.]

What's the right number? Nobody knows for sure! Yet the quality of care and patient safety experts when consulted all feel there are way too many patients either negligently harmed or needlessly dead and that crisis continues to go largely unreported or considered except by those who keep making estimates, while failing to establish definitive answers as to why. This quixotic dilemma led me to write the following thought paper.

The Lost Art of Asking Why?

Most, if not all, adults in their early years inundated their parents with, "Why Mommy?" "Why Daddy?" to the point of parental exasperation. Yet most adults lose that trait of seeking further clarification, particularly regarding issues of the highest importance. An example of this lack of rightfully inquisitive characteristic is, and long has been, occurring in the efforts to improve the quality of healthcare and patient safety.

Every new estimate of needless hospital deaths (NHD) annually has been greater than all previous estimates for the past twenty-five years, an indisputable fact, and a well-established track record of failure. But within Congress, every state legislature, and all forms of the national media, that established track record of failure makes all of the noise of a tree falling in an empty forest. Why?

Congress has established five agencies dedicated to improving the quality of healthcare, and patient safety; Joint Commission (1965) Agency for Healthcare Research and Quality (AHRQ), a division of DHHS (1989), Institute of Medicine (IOM)(now National Academy of Medicine) (1970), National Quality Forum (NQF), and Patient-Centered Outcomes Research Institute (PCORI) and three of those agencies has been functioning throughout that twenty-five year NHD track record of failure. But a visit to each of those agencies' web sites reveal no effort focused solely on that track record of failure. Why?

The latest estimate of NHDs reported in September 2013 was quadruple the 1990 estimate of 98,000 NHDs annually that was used in the IOM To Err Is Human report that promised to reduce that earlier estimate by 50% in five years. And that latest estimate was strongly supported, also in September 2013, by three nationally recognized patient safety experts, one of whom was a Co-Leader of the original 1990 report, and an active participant in the IOM To Err Is Human report. Both the IOM and Association of Health Care Journalists drop down lists of Selected Topics on their respective web sites fail to include needless hospital deaths.

There are a multitude of reasons contributing to why each estimate of NHDs has been greater than all previous estimates for the past twenty-five years, but those reasons are not being properly addressed. Statistics happen to someone else, but reality is personal. Needless hospital deaths do not occur in a vacuum, but they apparently occur in a system that lacks transparency, and they continue to fail to ignite national indignation. How many patients need to die needlessly in our nation's hospitals before that established track record of failure becomes a priority, and how many federal agencies supposedly created to address the quality of healthcare and patient safety will it take to finally achieve some resolution?

Needless hospital deaths, and negligent patient harm does occur in hospitals that are certified to exist by each state, and all of that patient harm, both fatal and non-fatal, is provided by doctors licensed in those states. But there is never any mention of each state's responsibility in the needless hospital deaths saga of failure. Again, Why?

"Why" should be a cogent question regarding the quarter century NHDs established track record of failure.

Question: How can a quarter century track record recorded in thousands of needless deaths continue to remain "under the radar" and with only the Hearst Newspapers attempt for national recognition of this enormous national disaster five years ago? Where is the outrage? While national decision-makers contest how to carve up the health care financial pie, thousands continue to die needlessly in our hospitals with less attention than is given to sporadic acts of needless deaths by violence at the hands of deranged individuals. When will NHDs receive the attention that crisis has long deserved?

I have read over four dozen books related to the quality of healthcare and patient safety, and none of those books recognize each state's responsibility to create and maintain an effective healthcare delivery system for their citizens, and none of them recognize what has long been recognized, that the current *system* is devoid of any systematic characteristics and therefore is a non-system. Therefore every person who claims they will provide greater patient safety by taking safety measures from existing systems, i.e. commercial aviation, nuclear industry, chemical industry, etc., and introduce such measures into the current Healthcare Delivery System are demonstrating their lack of understanding about that *system*. Their efforts will be like trying to put a square peg into a round hole. (See Appendix 4)

What did the Harvard Anesthesia Minimum Standards Really Demonstrate? Organized Structure, Authority, and Delegated Authority sufficient to provide Accountability

Harvard Medical School Department of Anesthesia clearly demonstrated everything that has always been missing in almost every element of the current healthcare delivery system thirty years ago. Because the patient safety need was so great in the nine hospital departments of anesthesia the Department leadership adopted the unthinkable in hospital medical staff management. They created, and enforced *minimum standards of care*, and the positive patient care results were immediate. The seven "lines in the sand" drawn by the Department leadership placed every medical practitioner under their authority that any deviation from those minimum standards would be judged to be inexcusable. Those minimum standards also demonstrated proof that clearly established authority could delegate sufficient authority to the nine hospital departments of anesthesia sufficient for effective accountability.

Harvard Medical School Department of Anesthesia demonstrated that it should not be necessary for each state to establish sufficient organizational structure throughout the current healthcare delivery system for meaningful accountability to take place. But unfortunately examples such as the Harvard Medical School Department of Anesthesia are the rare exceptions within the current healthcare delivery system, and the annual rate needless hospital deaths track record of failure is stark evidence.

Quality of Health Care and Patient Safety Army of experts has a track record that, I believe, can be summarized by three of the above quotes:

2000: IOM To Err Is Human: "Given current knowledge about the magnitude of the problem, the committee believe it would be irresponsible to expect anything less than a 50 percent reduction in errors over five years."

2008: NQF: Patient safety measures indicate that our nation is *improving in this area only 1 percent each year.*

2013 John James, PhD., Journal of Patient Safety, September: Estimated NHDs at more than 400,000 per year, and serious harm seems to be 10-t0-20-fold more common than lethal harm.

What's missing in all of the reports, studies, and estimates regarding needless hospital deaths during the past quarter century? There is no recognition, or reference to each state's responsibility regarding "never events" in their hospitals. In fact, no state is able to provide details, based upon facts regarding how many of those thousands of needless hospital deaths have occurred in their hospitals! Hospitals are the only place in America where an accidental death receives NO immediate review by a source of authority. And yet the decades-old crisis of needless hospital deaths continues to be ignored by decision makers in Congress, Federal Government, all 50 state governments and legislatures, Organized Medicine, and the Quality of Healthcare and Patient Safety army of experts.

Too many people continue to rave about To Err Is Human, and the other books in the IOM Crossing the Quality Chasm series. I have reviewed six of the seven books in that series, including To Err Is Human, and I consider the 53 recommendations contained in those six books I reviewed to be theoretical nonsense. Those 53 recommendations are a 20-page free down load on the second page of findtheblackbox.org web site.

Debates are, or should be, positive tools useful for imparting deeper understanding of important issues. Therefore I would welcome an opportunity to debate any person who would chose to attempt to defend the presumed benefits one might hope to take from To Err Is Human, and those 53 recommendations, which includes the nine recommendations found in To Err Is Human.

> **"You can avoid reality, but you cannot avoid the consequences of avoiding reality."**
> **Ayn Rand**

The entire Quality of Healthcare and Patient Safety Army of experts continue to ignore the realities of the Healthcare Delivery System; the absence of any systematic characteristics, and each state's responsibility to create and maintain an effective healthcare delivery system since all medical care is local and states license doctors. And while it is obvious that those six doctors I choose to illustrate the efforts of the Quality of Healthcare and Patient Safety Army of experts during the past several decades represent a very small portion of that army, those doctors, each in his own way, have been the "tip of the spear" in those efforts. One of the problems is that I appear to be the only person seeking to contribute to the efforts to improve the quality of healthcare and patient safety who has ever attempted to describe that army of experts in some detail.

Literally thousands of highly educated, and highly dedicated healthcare experts have been trying to improve the current Healthcare Delivery System while either failing to recognize both each state's responsibility to contribute to those efforts, and also the complete absence of an organizational structure absolutely necessary for points of authority and delegated authority necessary for meaningful accountability. Yet the relative size of that army of experts is like comparing a very large beach ball to a golf ball.

Perspective: One of the major problems in all of the attempts to improve the quality of healthcare and patient safety is that the world of Healthcare Cost & Access (how to pay for healthcare after-the-fact) dwarfs the world of the Quality of Healthcare and Patient Safety participants. Yet the quality of healthcare and patient safety can't be improved by cost manipulations, even though that tactic forms a major push by DHHS and CMS, and other healthcare agencies.

Regardless of that discrepancy the remainder of this book will focus on my view of what is necessary in order to begin to create a 21st century Healthcare Delivery System both worthy of that title, and worthy of this nation, and that is focused on how to improve the quality of healthcare and patient safety in every state.

CONCLUSION

Fact: The vast majority of medical care is acceptable, and much of it is exceptional. I know because I enjoy a high level of good health at my advanced age because of several successful major surgeries between 1962 and 2002. But the current Healthcare Delivery System is "broken", and has always been broken in its inability to properly respond to unacceptable patient care.

Consider these three tragic events that actually occurred at different times in my community.

First Event: A construction worker is accidentally killed at the work site. OSHA investigators are on the scene within hours.

Second Event: A single-engine airplane crashes on take off. Both occupants walk away with only slight injuries. FAA investigators are at the site within hours.

Third Event: A twenty-seven-year-old slender, healthy woman enters the hospital operating room for minor knee surgery under local anesthesia. She is injected once in the upper thigh area on the front and once in the buttocks. Within minutes, she suffers a catastrophic system collapse and within a few additional minutes *she is clinically dead!*

No investigators from any regulatory agency ever appeared at the site of that tragedy. Her widowed husband was forced to sue the doctors in order to find out what happened. *On the third anniversary of her death a lay jury returned a verdict of no negligence.* The doctors had won another court case.

Hospitals are the only site in America where an accidental death can occur and receive no regulatory, in-depth investigation. The practice of medicine is the least regulated economic activity. Both failures are the responsibility of state legislatures.

That series of events took place in or near our community twenty years ago, and nothing has changed the way such events are responded to in all three types of tragedies. If you or a loved one receives questionable patient care in any hospital in America no person with authority rapidly comes to investigate, and the hospital administrators and medical staff leadership goes into information lockdown, and the patient's family are left with Sue or Forget It. *Accountability* when bad things happen to patients is what has always been missing in every aspect of the current Healthcare Delivery System. And it is my belief, as stated above, that *both failures are the responsibility of state legislatures,* and governors of course.

Currently, there are three different systems that potentially can be used for the review of questionable patient care:

First, there are the state medical examining boards. Data from the Federation of State Medical Examining Boards show that system to rarely be used for the review of individual cases of questionable patient care. The potential for such use does exist, but in name only!

Second, there is medical peer review. Doctors reviewing the patient care of other doctors. Peer-review can occur at several levels of organized medicine, but the most effective system of medical peer review should occur at the hospital medical staff level. Does medical peer review occur at hospital medical staff's? Probably not! Why? Because Congress and the state legislatures made medical peer review totally secret! Medical peer review is more secret than almost anything else non-military. Yes, medical peer review does exist. But like fog, there is no discernible substance to medical peer review and no identifiable benefit to society. Medical peer review and the state medical examining board's review of questionable patient care both essentially exist in name only!

Third, there is the most obvious, medical malpractice litigation; the center of all public debate regarding questionable patient care. Sadly, if medical peer review functioned properly it would result in the need for far less medical malpractice litigation.

So, there exist three decidedly different systems with the potential ability to judge questionable patient care:

1. State medical examining boards are rarely if ever used to judge individual cases of questionable patient care.
2. Medical peer review is ultra-secret and there is no evidence in any city or town that the system functions to society's benefit.
3. Medical malpractice litigation (Sue or Forget It): there are countless articles and books detailing the laundry list of failures associated with this system.

Yet all three systems demand that the state board reviewers, medical peer review committee, and/or the civil court judge or jury create the medical standard of care they are to judge by.

And now for the central point of this discussion: the AMA definition of medical malpractice is treatment beneath the standard of care set by the law! Their words, not mine! So, where does that leave society? There can be no medical treatment given by a doctor to a patient without that treatment having a medical standard of care. Yet the AMA defines medical malpractice as *treatment beneath a standard of care set by the law.*

And people wonder why medical malpractice has been a major problem within our society for over 150 years. Doctors do not know how to judge other doctors! Yet there is NO medical malpractice without medical expert witness testimony. The root cause of the medical malpractice problem is created by that professional dilemma!

Until and unless doctors create a system whereby they can fairly judge other doctors regarding questionable patient care the medical malpractice crisis will continue to exist and continue to grow. Such a system whereby doctors can fairly judge other doctors without attorneys, courts and juries is far more attainable than imagined. I know because I can provide such a system.

Doctors created the medical malpractice litigation crisis by their failure to create a system whereby doctors (the best judges), could judge other doctors without attorneys, courts and juries. Thus society has always been left with Sue or Forget It! And attorneys filled the vacuum the doctors created by their own failure!

The AMA states, "The primary cause of America's medical liability crisis is overzealous personal injury attorneys who put their pocketbooks before patients."

Now ask yourself, if a person has surgery and in time reasonable questions arise, that happens, right, then "How, When and Where did an attorney create the problem?"

The AMA has no answer for that question. Doctors are the best judges of other doctors. But doctors don't know how to judge other doctors. And since Congress, all 50 state legislatures, and the AMA think that medical malpractice is treatment beneath a standard of care set by the law, then who cares?

Decades ago doctors failed to recognize the fatal flaw they were creating by not creating a system of medical peer review which could complement the marvelous scientific achievements of their profession. When doctors left society with Sue or Forget It, they drove a stake into the heart of their own profession. Only a system of medical peer review, fair to both doctor and patient, can ever right that wrong!

Our medical profession must redefine the definition of medical malpractice to treatment beneath a standard of care set by doctors, and not the law!

Each hospital medical staff should be considered the most important element in the current Healthcare Delivery System, and certainly in a 21st century Healthcare Delivery System. And if my premise becomes accepted, then how the members of each hospital medical staff comport themselves, both individually, and collectively, as either a truly professional organization, or just another group of doctors, each doing their own thing will send a clear message to their community.

Doctors assume the responsibility of seeking to treat the medical conditions of complete strangers, and strive to improve those individual's health, an awesome burden. And being human doctors, all doctors, will exhibit the human characteristics of falling short of perfection in their efforts of assuming that responsibility. When such failings occur, as they must, it becomes of the utmost importance as to how those doctors, both individually and collectively respond; in a truly professional manner, or not?

A 21st century Healthcare Delivery System must be based upon having medical peer review replace medical malpractice litigation (sue or forget it) as the primary system for the review of questionable patient care, and such review must take place where the event under review took place (hospitals) in the vast majority of cases.

Reality again: Thus far I have never found anyone who believes that members of any hospital medical staff in our nation are capable of implementing an effective system of medical peer review. But what does that deeply imbedded, negative assessment of all, or almost all, of the members of our medical profession say about doctors, and also say to both doctors and the public? I am well aware that the likelihood of any hospital medical staff creating such a system is most unlikely, but I still believe that IF the members of each hospital medical staff are challenged publicly by their communities some of those hospital medical staffs will choose to try to become true professionals.

Hospital medical staffs must be forced to become active partners with the people in their communities. Currently all evidence supports the understanding that the public has passively accepted the "fact" that no hospital medical staff should be expected to finally become the best judges of other doctors' questionable patient care issues, and I do not choose to accept that.

That is why I believe that Healthcare Warriors need to organize in every state and begin to demand that their Healthcare Delivery System begin to take on the attributes of a 21st century system, and also begin to demand that hospital medical staffs no longer be allowed to remain in their safe havens they have been so accustomed to for so long.

Would a system of medical peer review be difficult to establish? Yes! But would such a system of true professionalism be a game-changer? Yes! Either strive for something far better, or keep what you have now. First go back and read the New Jersey Law Revision Commission's description of medical peer review, and then ask if that is what your community deserves, and what some will begin to demand from their closest hospital medical staff. No hospital medical staff, administration, and board is going to voluntarily make such a transformational reconfiguration on their own, but such miraculous changes are necessary in order to create current century advancements.

I suggest that interested readers go back to Chapter 6 and reread what Professor Barzun said over 40 years ago about a true profession. The public only gets what it demands, and those demands, to be effective, must come from a unified source, I.e., Healthcare Warriors.

I am writing this in early April, and hope to have it available in the very near future. At the same time I am challenging a friend (perhaps former friend), and 6-term incumbent for his seat in the South Carolina House of Representatives. The primary is scheduled for June 13, and there are three candidates for that office, therefore a primary runoff "might" be necessary, but regardless of the outcome of that political race I will be actively seeking individuals who would be interested in becoming sufficiently organized to begin to make a major difference in their Healthcare Delivery System.

An additional note: I am quite possibly the oldest successful surgical expert witness on record. Last year a judge in California accepted my multi-page Declaration that caused an oral & maxillofacial surgeon, his attorney, and his insurance company to satisfactory settle their surgical malpractice case with a young, Muslin attorney who that surgeon had permanently harmed in, not one, but two surgeries, and the second of those surgeries should have been unnecessary. I say this in the further hope of reassuring any person interested in joining me in an effort to make their and their loved one's Healthcare Delivery System far better. And I close with the following consideration.

A Cautionary Tale:

Former South Carolina Governor Nikki Haley will be credited with numerous positive accomplishments during her term in office, but regarding the Healthcare Delivery System she was incompetent, and not just because I say so. I told her during her first year in office that two of the top healthcare experts had stated publicly that the current system was broken, and also that I could provide her with a logical and doable process to begin to improve that system, and her response was, "I can't". But there is more. During her first year in office other experts were warning that multiple rural hospitals were facing dire circumstances, and again she did nothing. By the time she left office, three rural hospitals had closed, and others remained in jeopardy. Furthermore, during her six State-of-the-State presentations Education received significant consideration in all six events while ObamaCare forced her to speak about a possible Healthcare Exchange in one presentation and a very brief comment regarding healthcare in the next presentation for a total of perhaps ten minutes or less. The Cautionary Tale is that people in every state who care about their and their loved ones' Healthcare Delivery System should seek to ascertain where their system is on their governor's and state legislature's priority list. South Carolina's Legislature has 27 Standing Committees, 14 Senate, 13 House, and the word Healthcare does not appear on the page. I anticipate that every other state will demonstrate similar Healthcare Delivery System shortcomings.

Healthcare Warriors requires activists who seek to become students of their and their loved ones Healthcare Delivery System, therefore those who might think I have provided far more information about our current system, and how it has evolved in such a haphazard manner is too much information might want to refocus on what all of the current experts have been trying to tell the nation, and its leaders for the past several decades. One should never try to substantially change an enormous, complex system without first asking, and answering the question; where are we now, and how did we get here?

I can guide activists who are willing to dedicate their efforts toward seeking a far better Healthcare Delivery System for themselves, and their loved ones on how to begin to ask, and answer that critical question.

ABOUT DR. WILLIAMS

Author:
Find The Black Box, Prevent Needless Hospital Deaths, 2013
Misdiagnosed, Why Current Health Care Change Is Malpractice, 2010
First Do No Harm, The Cure for Medical Malpractice, 2004

Consultant:
Dr. Williams remains active as a surgical malpractice expert witness and medical peer review expert.

Professional:
Board certified oral & maxillofacial surgeon and anesthesiologist.
President, Wisconsin Society Oral & Maxillofacial Surgeons 1977-78
Chairman, Dental Department and Member, Executive Committee, Medical Staff, Methodist Hospital, Madison, Wis. 1974-76 1980-82

Military:
USAF retired major, senior navigator/bombardier.
Commanding Officer, Headquarters Squadron, 461st Bomb Wing, Blytheville, AFB AK (also Summary Court Martial Officer) 1956-57

Assigned to Tactical Bomb Wings as navigator-bombardier in Korea, Florida, Texas, South Carolina, Louisiana and Arkansas 1954-57

U.S. Air Force Reserve 702nd Troop Carrier Sq. Memphis, TN 1957

Activated back into the U.S.A.F. Cuban Crisis Oct. 1962

President Kennedy awarded Presidential Unit Citation 1962

Combat ready in three different types of combat aircraft.

MY BOOKS

Healthcare Warriors, Why and How to Become One, 2018
Find The Black Box, Prevent Needless Hospital Deaths 2013
Misdiagnosed, Why Current Health Care Change Is Malpractice 2010
First Do No Harm, The Cure for Medical Malpractice 2004

Other Books I have read and are in my possession

2019 These 4 new additions to my list.
Semmelweis, His Life and His Doctrine – Sir William Tapp Sinclair 2018
Louis Pasteur – Patrice DeBre' – Translated by Elborg Forster 1994
The Butchering Art, Joseph Lister's Quest to Transform the Grisly World of Vic. Med. Lindsey Fitzharris 2017
Dr. Mutter's Marvels = Cristin O'Keefe Aptowicz 2014

Unaccountable – Dr. Marty Makary 2012 (This book caused me to write Find The Black Box 2013

Being Mortal – Dr. Atul Gawande - 2014
The Checklist Manifesto – Dr. Atul Gawande – 2010
Better – Dr. Atul Gawande – 2007
Complications – Dr. Atul Gawande – 2002
Mistreated – Dr. Robert Pearl – 2017
Malpractice – Dr. Lawrence Schlachter - 2017

Beyond the Checklist – Suzanne Gordon, Pat Mendenhall, Bonnie O'Conner – 2013

The Truth About Big Medicine – Cheryl Brown & John James - 2015

Principles & Practice of Clinical Research 3rd Ed. 2012 Edited by John I. Gallin, FrederickP. Ognibene

Service Fanatics – Dr. James Merlino – 2015

Doctor, Your Patient Will See You Now, Dr. Steven Kussin – 2011

Designed to Adapt – Dr. John Kenagy – 2009

Internal Bleeding – Robert Wachter, MD, Kaveh Shojania, MD – 2004

Severed Trust – Dr. George Lundberg – 2000

W. Edwards Deming – Cecelia S. Kilian - 1992

Institute of Medicine's Quality Chasm series – 53 recommendations
    To Err Is Human – 2000 – 9 recommendations
    Crossing the Quality Chasm – 2001 – 13 recommendations
    Leadership by Example – 2002 – 8 recommendations
    Health Professions Education – 2003 – 10 recommendations
    Priority Areas for National Action – 2003 – 6 recommendations
    Patient Safety – 2004 – 7 recommendations

Improving Diagnosis in Medicine IOM 2015
The Healthcare Imperative IOM 2010
Delivering Health Care, A Systems Approach, L. Shi & D. A. Singh 5th Edition 2012

The Company That Saved Heath Care – John Torinus, Jr. - 2010

The Social Transformation of American Medicine – Paul Starr – 1982

Healthcare Delivery in the U.S. 10th Ed. 2011 Anthony R. Kovner & James R. Knickman

Medical Quality Management 2010 Editor Prathibha Varkey, M.D. Am. College of Medical Quality

DHHS/OIG External Review of Hospital Quality by Joint Commission 1999

We CAN Fix Healthcare – Dr. Stephen Klasko, G. Shea, M. Hoad, - 2016

The Doctor Crisis – Jack Cochran, MD, Charles Kenney – 2014

Surviving Your Doctors – Dr. Richard Klein – 2010

Flatlined Guy L. Clifton, M.D. 2011

Escape Fire Donald M. Berwick 2004
Through The Patient's Eyes – Picker/Commonwealth Program – 1993 (Dr. Berwick)
Curing Health Care – Don Berwick, A. B. Godfrey, J Roessner – 1990 - 2002

Wall of Silence – Rosemary Gibson, J. P. Singh - 2003

The Empowered Patient – Dr. Julia Hallisy – 2008

The Soul of Medicine – Dr. Sherwin Nuland – 2009
Doctors Sherwin B. Nuland 1988

How Doctors Think – Dr. Jerome Groopman - 2007

Where Does It Hurt? – Jonathan Bush – 2014

Who Killed Health Care? – Regina Herzlinger – 2007

One Nation – Dr. Ben Carson – 2014

The System – Haynes Johnson, David Broder - 1996

The Collapse of the Common Good – Phillip Howard - 2001

Highest Duty – "Sully" Sullenberger - 2010

Gesundheit! – Dr. Patch Adams – 1993 – 1998

Healing America – Dr/Senator William Frist – 2004

The Lost Art of Healing – Dr. Bernard Lown – 1996

Madame Curie – Eve Curie – 1938
Marie Curie – Susan Quinn - 1995

Iconoclast, Abraham Flexner & a Life in Learning, Thomas Neville Bonner 2002
Abraham Flexner, A Flawed American Icon Michael Nevins - 2010

Einstein's Greatest Mistake, David Bodanis, 2016

The Greater Journey – Americans in Paris – David McCullough - 2011

Physical Diagnosis 17th Ed. – J. W. Burnside, T. J. McGlynn – 1987

The HCAHPS Handbook – Quint Studer - 2010

Code of Medical Ethics – AMA – 2000-2001 Ed/

Professing Medicine – AMA – 2002

Journal of Legal Medicine – So. Ill. Un. School of Law – 2003

Constitution & Bylaws of the AMA – 2004

Legal Medicine 5th Ed. – American College of Legal Medicine – 2001

Credentialing & Privileging Your Medical Staff – Joint Commission – 2007

The Medical Staff Handbook – Joint Commission – 2004

US ARMED FORCES – Nuclear, Biological & Chemical Survival Manual – 2003

The Truth About Big Medicine – Cheryl Brown, John James & contributions by; Yanling Yu, PhD - Robert E. Oshel, PhD – Gerald Rogan, MD - Stephen S. Tower, MD - Daniel M. Saman, DrPH, MPH, CPH - Evelyn V. McKnight, AuD - Lisa McGiffert - Denise Lasater, DBA, RN - Kiran Sagar, MD, FAHA, FACC

www.ingramcontent.com/pod-product-compliance
Lightning Source LLC
LaVergne TN
LVHW092050060526
838201LV00047B/1326